Between the blaring, always-on-duty world of mothering and our woman's wistful yearning for personal time and space, Mandy Arioto wedges a place for us to *be*. Courageous. Ever honest. Present. Here is a lovely read that weaves hope in our *here*. I found myself bobbing along after Mandy's musings, chasing her like a child after a firefly through inky nights, eager to capture her discoveries as my own. Dark. Light. Mandy convinces us that God uses *everything* to shape us into who we always wanted to be.

—ELISA MORGAN, speaker, author, *The Beauty of Broken* and *Hello, Beauty Full*; cohost, *Discover the Word*, www.discovertheword.org; President Emerita, MOPS International, www.mops.org

Starry-Eyed will encourage moms of all ages and stages to embrace grace in the midst of their ordinary life. From the weary to the wonderful, the stressful to the sublime, God is there. We just need a little help seeing him. Mandy Arioto shows us how.

—KAREN EHMAN, *New York Times* bestselling author of *Keep It Shut* and *Hoodwinked*; Proverbs 31 Ministries speaker; wife and mother of three

Mandy's candid stories about what it means to be a woman, a wife, and a mother had me laughing out loud one moment and crying the next. *Starry-Eyed* is the kind of book you buy multiple copies of to give away to friends.

—JJ HELLER, singer/songwriter

I first heard of Mandy when I was a pastor at MOSAIC in Los Angeles. Our campus pastor in San Diego kept saying, "You have to meet Mandy!" He would tell me, "She's the future, man." I finally got to know Mandy in an RV by the beach on a "speaker's retreat" that turned into a surf session. I was struck by her quiet power and her depth of insight. When Mandy leads, people grow. When Mandy speaks, hearts open. When Mandy cares, our world heals. Mandy is an amazing mom, leader, speaker, and woman of faith. As I read Mandy's book, I thought of my own mom, my wife, my sisters, and my daughters. I want them to be informed by Mandy's bold and insightful words. I want my daughters to know they were created for the wild light and the beautiful darkness. I'm getting this book for every mom in my life.

—HANK FORTENER, founder, AdoptTogether.org; teaching
pastor, MOSAIC

By dignifying the darkness, Mandy Arioto leads us into the dark night as well as the jubilant light and reminds us there are gifts in both. Whether she's writing about motherhood, vocation, friendship, marriage, or family, we are invited to consider how we are formed by life's changing skies. You are sure to find yourself and your journey in these pages.

—LEEANA TANKERSLEY, author of *Brazen* and *Breathing Room*

Starry-Eyed

Starry-Eyed

Seeing Grace in the Unfolding
Constellation of Life and Motherhood

MANDY ARIOTO

ZONDERVAN

Starry-Eyed
Copyright © 2016 by MOPS International, Inc.

Requests for information should be addressed to:
Zondervan, 3900 Sparks Dr. SE, Grand Rapids, Michigan 49546

ISBN 978-0-310-34036-2 (ebook)

Library of Congress Cataloging-in-Publication Data

Names: Arioto, Mandy, author.
Title: Starry-eyed : seeing grace in the unfolding constellation of life and motherhood / Mandy Arioto.
Description: Grand Rapids : Zondervan, 2016.
Identifiers: LCCN 2015044542 | ISBN 9780310340409 (softcover)
Subjects: LCSH: Mothers — Religious life. | Motherhood — Religious aspects — Christianity.
Classification: LCC BV4529.18 .A75 2016 | DDC 248.8/431 — dc23 LC record available at http://lccn.loc.gov/2015044542

Excerpt from *Blessings for the Fast Paced and Cyberspaced: Parables, Reflections and Prayers*, 2nd ed. (Phoenix: Tau Publishing, 2011) by William John Fitzgerald, ©2000. Used with permission.

Excerpt from *The Circle of Life* by Joyce Rupp and Macrina Wiederkehr, ©2005. Used with permission of the publisher, Sorin Books®, an imprint of Ava Maria Press®, Inc., P. O. Box 428, Notre Dame, IN 46556, www.sorinbooks.com.

Excerpt from "Our Vanishing Night," *National Geographic*, November 2008 by Verlyn Klinkenborg. Used with permission.

All Scripture quotations, unless otherwise indicated, are taken from the Holy Bible, New International Version®, NIV®. Copyright © 1973, 1978, 1984, 2011 by Biblica, Inc.® Used by permission of Zondervan. All rights reserved worldwide. www.Zondervan.com. The "NIV" and "New International Version" are trademarks registered in the United States Patent and Trademark Office by Biblica, Inc.®

Any Internet addresses (websites, blogs, etc.) and telephone numbers in this book are offered as a resource. They are not intended in any way to be or imply an endorsement by Zondervan, nor does Zondervan vouch for the content of these sites and numbers for the life of this book.

All rights reserved. No part of this publication may be reproduced, stored in a retrieval system, or transmitted in any form or by any means—electronic, mechanical, photocopy, recording, or any other—except for brief quotations in printed reviews, without the prior permission of the publisher.

Cover design: Curt Diepenhorst
Interior design: Denise Froehlich

First printing February 2016 / Printed in the United States of America

For Cindy and Charley:
"Our roots will always be tangled. I am glad for that."[1]

And for the A-team:
Joe, Joseph, Ellie, and Charlotte

---

1   Ally Condie, *Matched* (New York: Speak, 2011), 216.

Contents

Introduction: With Stars in Our Eyes 11

1. SWELL SEASONS:
   When Motherhood is Like the Ocean 17
2. BLESSING THE NIGHT:
   Embracing the Riches in Darkness. 23
3. BECOMING MY MOTHER:
   A Reason to Dance. 31
4. TOGETHER, WE'VE GOT THIS:
   Sister Courage and Borrowed Light 36
5. DEAR FIFTEEN:
   Permission to Sit with Our Pain. 43
6. HE HAD ME AT "UGH":
   Joe, Marriage, and Creating a Legacy 50
7. IN THE BELLY OF THE HOLY ONE:
   Birthing a New Concept of God. 55
8. CONFIDENCE OVER CONFORMITY:
   Reclaiming Our Birthrights 60
9. BREATHING IN THE LIGHT:
   Drawing Inspiration from the People around Us 67
10. MAGIC IN BROOKLYN:
    Cultivating Timeless Delight 71
11. SABBATH LIKE A SUNRISE:
    Restoring Our Weary Places 77
12. THE WOMB TIME THAT WINTER BRINGS:
    Surrendering to Nature's Rhythms. 85

13. A CONSTELLATION OF REASONS:
Extracting Truth from the Natural World 93

14. SENSUALITY:
Becoming Comfortable in Our Own Skin 102

15. FEMININE POWER:
What I Will Teach My Girls about Being a Woman 110

16. THE LIGHT OVER THE DINNER TABLE:
Cultivating a Hospitable Heart. 114

17. THE BUS STOP:
Things Are Always More than Meet the Eye. 118

18. THE POWER OF STORY:
Illuminating Meaning for One Another 125

19. THE EYES HAVE IT:
Celebrating a Worthy Calling. 131

20. TO LIVE LIKE MUSIC:
Learning to Feel All Our Feelings 135

21. FAILING GLORIOUSLY:
Redefining Success and Failure 141

22. BANISHING OUR GHOSTS:
Confronting the Shame That Holds Us Captive 146

23. CONFESSIONALS:
Finding the Courage to Be Honest 154

24. EARMUFFS AND BACHELORS:
Teaching My Kids about Hearing God 162

25. FORGET-ME-NOTS:
Hope Looks like Despair 169

26. A DAZZLING UNFOLDING:
The Process of Becoming Ourselves. 174

27. STARRY NIGHT:
When the Next Step Is Uncertain 178

28. GOOD THINGS RUN WILD:
The Kingdom Comes. 184

Acknowledgments 189

Introduction:
With Stars in Our Eyes

Have you ever had a time in your life when things felt off? Like the sun has become eclipsed by the moon and everything that at one point made sense in the bright light of day now feels uncertain in its darkness?

There are three distinct seasons in my life when I forgot what the warmth of light felt like; three seasons when uncertainty consumed and I had to learn how to make peace with the dark. The first was when I was twenty and was confronted with a loss that took the breath out of my lungs, the second was a season when I was searching for what I was supposed to do in the world, and the last one happened on a warm night one May.

The night was unusually humid for spring in Northern California. The evening breeze that blew through my hair and over my bare shoulders was just enough to make being outside bearable. My three-year-old son and I were standing in our driveway just like we did every night that spring, under a dark sky filled with stars. Each night we followed the same routine. Just before bed, Joseph and I would grab hands and walk outside to stand in our driveway. He would find the moon, and then we would both point out the stars and constellations whose lights were beginning to emerge as the darkness deepened. Holding his hand, I could feel the beat of his heart straight through our meshed fingers. We were connected not only by blood

11

but also because we had once shared the most intimate space for nine months. Our hearts were synced to one another's.

On this particular night I was heartbroken. Joe and I had been trying for seven months to get pregnant with a second child, but once again my body bled, and disappointment plunged me into a desolation that was becoming all too familiar. Sensing my despair, my husband Joe joined us in the driveway. He wrapped his arm around my waist and whispered that everything would be okay, and that a family of three can be just as awesome as a family of four. Then, in a gesture to brighten the mood, he pulled out some matches along with a long, thin box of sparklers I had been storing away for the Fourth of July.

He handed our three-year-old a sparkler, struck a match against the sidewalk, and lit the silver stick in Joseph's tiny, anxious hand. The sparkler began flickering and hissing. Sparks flew, illuminating the darkness right around us. As I kneeled down next to my son in order to take it all in, I noticed that instead of watching the light in his hands, he was looking straight into my eyes. He waved the sparkler from side to side but kept his gaze focused on me. I watched him for a few minutes, curious as to why the sparklers weren't holding his attention. Then he said it.

"Momma, I see stars in your eyes."

Glittering sparks, just like the flickering stars we gazed at every night, were reflected in my eyes. That moment was the start of my awakening to the fact that glimmers of light were shining in my darkness if only I trained my eyes to see them.

It was the beginning of a journey toward becoming starry-eyed.

This book is a collection of essays about light and darkness, hope and heartache, brokenness and wholeness, and what to do when you don't know what to do. It is meant to be a north star for all of us travelers, reminding us that Someone has gone ahead of us and left glimmering lights to help guide us home.

One of my favorite constellations is the Pleiades, also called the Seven Sisters. It is one of the nearest star clusters to Earth and the most visible to the naked eye. Legend says that the Pleiades were the seven daughters of Atlas, the giant who bears the world upon his shoulders. These seven maidens were transformed into stars because of their "amiable virtues and mutual affection" and because Orion was constantly wooing them, which caused them great discomfort.[1] They appealed for help to Zeus, the overseer of all the gods, and out of pity for them he changed them into doves. As doves they then flew up into the sky and found a hiding place among the stars.

I like the idea of finding a hiding place among the stars, of finding home amongst the brilliant light and darkest night. As we look at the night sky of our own lives, patterns begin to emerge. We start to notice swirling constellations making beautiful configurations that we can see clearly only in the dark.

Carl Jung suggests that becoming whole means bringing together that which has been torn apart.[2] Whether that is light and darkness, feminine and masculine, conscious and unconscious, we are whole when we embrace both. In fact, the whole universe unfolds through paired opposites—sun and moon, hot and cold, black and white. I love women who have chosen to bring together the light and dark in their lives and make peace with all of it. Not only are they more compassionate but they are also the ones who change the world. They are the ones who aren't afraid of being honest about their flaws and fears and who are eager to reflect sparks of hope and love to the people around them.

---

1   "Miscellaneous Notes and Queries, with Answers," *Notes and Queries and Historic Magazine: A Monthly of History, Folk-lore, Mathematics, Literature, Science, Art, Arcane Societies, Etc.* 3–4 (1886–87): 401.

2   As discussed in R. Frager and J. Fadiman, *Personality and Personal Growth*, 6th ed. (New York: Pearson Prentice Hall, 2005), 56.

As you read the pages ahead, think of each essay as a star in the sky, each contributing to a beautiful constellation that makes up your life in all its darkness and light. Bring these words along with you to the park and on the subway and even into the bathroom as you steal away for a few minutes to yourself. It may take a little time to adjust your eyes and soul to see the goodness in both the light and darkness of life and motherhood, but as you do, you may find yourself transformed into a dove, hidden safely in the Creator's night sky.

I think it is seriously cool that we all get to do life together, sharing the pretty and painful all mingled together in a way that creates something whole and beautiful. Thank you for holding my messes and triumphs gently and with palms wide open to whatever it is a few words in a little book can offer.

With hearts on sleeves and sparklers in hand, may we all see glittering lights in the darkness. May we become starry-eyed. Together.

P.S. A wise friend once told me that they refused to participate in Q & As, also known as question-and-answer sessions. Instead they preferred Q & Rs, question and responses. This idea stuck with me, because as far as I can tell, we are all questioning and responding most of our lives. And the idea that there is one right answer leaves me uncomfortable and with a little bit of performance anxiety. So at the end of each chapter you will find a section for Q & R. There are no right or wrong answers, only what is the most true for you at this very moment in life. Grab some friends and spill your guts, or work through them in a journal by yourself. However you choose to engage these questions, be open to how your eyes may be adjusting to a new form of illumination that is both holy and unexpected.

Q & R

1. Look back over your life and reflect on the experiences that seemed dark, painful, or uncertain. Try to draw your personal "constellation" of major positive and negative experiences in your journal.

2. As you reflect on your life, what patterns and seasons of light and dark do you see?

3. Where are you longing for some illumination today—right at this moment?

* * *

CHAPTER 1

Swell Seasons:
When Motherhood Is
Like the Ocean

As moms, we all know that we would do anything for our kids. But today I truly took one for my team. I crawled under the door of a public restroom stall because my youngest daughter had insisted on going in by herself, which of course meant locking the door. She then yelled to me that she needed help, which is not easily accomplished when Mom is on the other side of the door, and said child will not hop off the potty to unlock the door. After what seemed like hours of negotiations, the only option was to crawl under the stall door. That's right—hands and knees on the floor, followed by soldier crawl on my tummy, to find my little one smiling at me from her perch on the potty. Hours later, I contemplated another option I didn't think of at the time: I could have crawled over the stall. A bit precarious, but certainly more sanitary than the floor crawl I hastily chose as my only option.

I share this story to document, for my kids, the depth of my love for them. Soldier-crawl-on-public-bathroom-floor = laying your life down for your child.

This motherhood deal is a pretty classy gig.

There are so many things that have surprised me about being a mom. Like how crawling on the floor of a public restroom would ever be a consideration. Or how decentering having a baby can be, yet how wholly I would want to give myself to another. Another thing that surprised me is the saturation of feeling that would flood me at unexpected times.

Motherhood reminds me of playing in the ocean. Like when I was in high school and we spent most of our summer days at the beach. We would wake up late, and if we had spent the night at Michelle's we would eat peanut butter swirl ice cream for brunch. Then we'd pile too many people into someone's mom's minivan and head to Oceanside for an afternoon in the sand. We would oil our skin, bronze until we blistered (I know, I know), and then run to the water to cool off. The waves made for a great diversion from all the boy watching and red-vine licorice eating.

In order to really experience the waves, we would swim out as far as possible while still touching the bottom; then we'd wait for the biggest ones to roll in. The game was to try to jump over the waves without getting knocked back to shore. If a wave was powerful enough, and you chose to jump, the swell would sweep your feet out from under you. You would get tossed around a bit and inhale some water up your nose until you regained your footing, just in time for the next wave. The goals were to keep your balance, to laugh like crazy when you lost it, and to avoid exposing your booty to the entire shoreline when your swimsuit bottom got rearranged in the surf.

Being a mom is like high school at the beach; I am constantly being moved by swells that threaten my footing.

Some of us are initiated into motherhood with an inner knowing. We are the ones who notice the first flutter of life inside us. We carry our children for months and know them before anyone else does. Others of us come to motherhood with an inner knowing that our child is to be welcomed from an external place, where we labor for years with hope and paperwork to welcome them into our family. How we arrive at motherhood has no bearing on the fact that it is filled with seasons made up of the brightest and also the darkest of days.

Darkness is immediate. Our bellies swell, or our hearts are knit together in the dark of another's womb. We rock and feed babies in the dark. For some of us postpartum depression is the pitchest black we have ever known. From the dark womb we welcome new life, and our own new life, a life we haven't known, unfolds before us as well. The unknown can feel uncertain with its shadows.

Daylight comes, as it always does, and we feel a little more equipped to face the new swells. Time goes by and we realize we are enjoying ourselves. We laugh at what once overwhelmed us, and we welcome firsts without so much fear.

First tooth, first step, first word. First day of preschool.

We laugh with our friends about how growing a baby took nine months, but bedtime takes for-freaking-ever.

Motherhood is full of joy, full of moments that make you relish who you are becoming. You give and give, and it's okay because there is no shortage of love in your starry depths. Until it is infuriating as all get-out because you can't reason with a four-year-old crazy person who, once all sweetness, is now screaming at you because she wanted the cherry sucker, not the stupid grape one. Bless her heart.

Your nighttime watch comes round again. You sit with a child whose fever is raging like fire, his hot breath on your neck. Your arms are tired, not from the holding but from the weariness that threatens to pin you to the floor. Tears swell. Worry and exhaustion make the night feel long and lonely.

The fever breaks, and relief washes over you. The light returns. Bedtime still takes for-freaking-ever, but that is okay because motherhood is made up of hard and beautiful moments that come together to create some pretty swell seasons.

Sun and inky blue water. Light and darkness at the same time.

I remember one time when my mom told me she dreamed my brother and I were little again, and we were all under her roof. She said she cried when she woke up and realized it was only a dream.

When we are in the midst of mothering our children, believing that it is all good is difficult. And it is difficult, but also thrilling.

One thing I have learned in my thirteen years of being a mom (I know what you are thinking, I couldn't possibly be old enough to have a thirteen-year-old; you're right, and I love you) is that we miss out on the fun because of our expectations. Thoughts that sweep our feet out from under us are, "I thought I would be a better mom; I thought my birth story would be different; I don't feel as happy as I thought I would; I can't do it all."

Not being able to do it all is my shame trigger. And I am one of those really bad jugglers. I disappoint people and I forget my nephew's birthday and I miss deadlines. It is in my bad juggling moments, when I can't attain my self-imposed standard of perfection, that I feel like a complete failure—even though my nephew eventually gets a present, and the assignment gets turned in a few days late. It has taken a lot of years and some therapy to realize that my idea of perfection is a myth. It is completely unattainable. And trying to live at an unattainable pace has sucked all the fun right out of my soul more often than I care to admit.

For me, the trick of regaining my perspective and joy in mothering is permission to live freer. Free from clenched hands. Free not to always need to be in control. Free to do life my own way, not how everyone else is doing it. And free from being held hostage by the myth of perfection. Have you ever noticed how perfection looks good with her shiny manicure and homemade kombucha, but really she is the snob that no one wants to invite to their BBQ? The reason is perfection is annoying and frankly no fun. I find perfection is at best an illusion and at worst a lie. And this whole concept of defining success as the ability to balance everything only makes sense if you are a juggler in the circus.

Being a mom is all of it. Light and dark, joy, frustration, and consuming love. I think Debra Ginsberg had it right when she said, "Through the blur, I wondered if I was alone or if other parents felt the same way I did—that everything involving our children was painful in some way. The emotions, whether they were joy, sorrow, love or pride, were so deep and sharp that in the end they left you raw, exposed and yes, in pain."[1]

For the rest of my life, I will be wading in the swells. I will feel it all deeply—the moments of darkness and the blindingly beautiful light. I will mess up and succeed—both many times over. Through all the swells there will be something holy, like a mother, putting breath back into lungs and holding close so there is no doubt about the depth of love surrounding it all: this fierce, fragile, thrilling, midnight motherhood.

Whatever season you are in—waiting for a baby, hoping for a mate, sending kids to college, or beginning a new adventure—may part of your story be about trusting that the swells are part of the game. And that jumping in is always worth it.

Q & R

1. Which of these shame triggers around mothering resonate with you? "I thought I'd be better at mothering." "I wanted a different birth story." "I don't feel as happy as I thought I would." "I thought I'd be able to do it all."

---

1   Debra Ginsberg, *Raising Blaze: A Mother and Son's Long, Strange Journey into Autism* (New York: Harper Perennial, 2003), 188.

2. Write your own personal definition of "successful mothering."

3. How does perfectionism show up in your life? What does that look like and what are the effects?

4. What might you let go of that would leave you feeling freer as a mom?

* * *

CHAPTER 2

Blessing the Night:
Embracing the Riches
in Darkness

For a few years during my childhood, I lived on a small horse farm in upstate New York. On summer nights, my friend Kate and I would sneak out of the house and tiptoe barefoot through the dewy grass to the hill just in front of the big red barn. This was our spot. The place where we would lie under the stars without the intrusion of manmade light. In our childhood innocence we believed we had found a secret spot where the stars shone brighter than anywhere else. A secret between us and the sky, where the stars told us truths they didn't share with anyone else.

As a grown woman, I now know it was the lack of city lights that made the stars so much more brilliant, but the magic of those moments hasn't left me. In fact, I still feel the same two powerful sensations when I lie in the grass to gaze at the night sky as I did on those warm nights in front of the barn. The first is a sense of connection to creation, a universal experience of the holy that I still have trouble putting into words; the second is a feeling of insignificance. Under the vastness of the evening sky, I am overwhelmed by the smallness of my experiences compared to the galaxies beyond what my eyes can see. I am reminded that my world is infinitely bigger than the four walls of my house, and that I am not the center of any universe.

Often we lose such a perspective, content to sit under our plastered ceilings, mindlessly slipping into a narrow belief that what happens within the walls we call home is, in fact, the universe itself. This kind of thinking makes our world smaller and smaller. Crowded. Suffocating. Eventually we become trapped by our own puny logic, satisfied to limit our lives to the things we can understand with our cerebral cortex.

We forget how to be awed.

I believe that many of the most life-giving moments take place in the moonlight.

My very first kiss happened under a sky full of stars in the driveway of my house. Nearly every one of the best celebrations that I have been a part of culminated in dancing long into the night. All three of my babies were born under a night sky. I fell in love with my husband Joe over long talks lit by the moon. And yet so many of my beliefs about darkness reverberate with negative associations.

As a kid—and, let's be honest, even sometimes as an adult—I felt the need to have a light on as I slept so as to avoid waking up to pitch black. Now, when my emotions feel dark, I run as fast as I can to my therapist or my mom, looking for perspective to talk myself out of the gloom. Late one night when a work meeting downtown lasted well past dusk, I walked to the parking garage with keys in my hand, just in case I needed to defend myself.

In spite of all the wonders that I have experienced in the dark, in many cases it still feels dangerous. But I am made to live by both moonlight and sunlight. I am designed to live fully in all gradations of illumination without fear, knowing that the nighttime half can be just as compelling as the daytime.

The necessity of darkness in our lives is literally a matter of biology. Darkness is as essential to our physical well-being as light. I have a friend who endured extensive military training for potential torture scenarios in case he was captured in a hostile situation. For the first part of the training, over the span of a single weekend, he was put in a pitch-dark cell by himself. He recalls losing all sense of time and wondering if he would ever see the light again. During the second part of the weekend, he was forced to sit under artificial light for an extended period of time. He said the light caused even more stress and confusion than the darkness. He no longer had any external cues to maintain his body's natural rhythm.

Just as solitary confinement in the dark is used as a form of torture, so is exposure to unending light. Human beings exposed only to light will experience extreme emotional duress. Darkness is a necessary part of emotional and physical health; we cannot function normally without it.

In a *National Geographic* article entitled "Our Vanishing Night," Verlyn Klinkenborg writes about our biological need for darkness:

> Unlike astronomers, most of us may not need an undiminished view of the night sky for our work, but like most other creatures we do need darkness. Darkness is as essential to our biological welfare, to our internal clockwork, as light itself. The regular oscillation of waking and sleep in our lives—one of our circadian rhythms—is nothing less than a biological expression of the regular oscillation of light on Earth. So fundamental are these rhythms to our being that altering them is like altering gravity.
>
> For the past century or so, we've been performing an open-ended experiment on ourselves, extending the day, shortening the night, and short-circuiting the human body's sensitive response to light. The consequences of our bright new world are more readily perceptible in less adaptable creatures living in the peripheral glow of our prosperity. But for humans, too, light pollution may take a biological toll. At least one new study has suggested a direct correlation between higher rates of

breast cancer in women and the nighttime brightness of their neighborhoods.

In the end, humans are no less trapped by light pollution than the frogs in a pond near a brightly lit highway. Living in a glare of our own making, we have cut ourselves off from our evolutionary and cultural patrimony—the light of the stars and the rhythms of day and night. In a very real sense, light pollution causes us to lose sight of our true place in the universe, to forget the scale of our being, which is best measured against the dimensions of a deep night with the Milky Way—the edge of our galaxy—arching overhead.[1]

We live in a world that spins intentionally to a rhythm of daylight and moonlight. Instead of trying to outrun darkness or navigate around it, perhaps we need to recognize our dependence upon it—and to name it good.

In the beginning of God's story in the world, we read a creation poem that illuminates the origins of darkness. We read that the earth is formless and empty, and darkness is over the surface of the deep. God separates the light from the darkness, then creates the sun and moon and declares, "It is good." This means that "good" is both light and darkness, not either-or.

Once darkness and light are blessed by the Creator, we read, "And there was evening, and there was morning—the first day" (Gen 1:5). The first evening was followed by the first morning, and thus a rhythm was given to our twenty-four hours. I like the idea that the first day started at night. In the Hebrew understanding of time, each day begins not with the morning, but with the night. When three stars are visible in the night sky, the next day officially begins. This begs the question: Does darkness extinguish light, or does light emerge from darkness?

---

1   "Our Vanishing Night," *National Geographic*, November 2008, http://ngm.national-geographic.com/print/2008/11/light-pollution/klinkenborg-text. Used with permission.

In her book *Learning to Walk in the Dark*, Barbara Brown Taylor writes that "new life starts in the dark. Whether it is a seed in the ground, a baby in the womb, or Jesus in the tomb, it starts in the dark."[2] Even the cycle of Earth's year starts with the winter solstice. In this time of greatest darkness, humanity waits for the birth of a new year and the new life that has been hibernating in the dark of winter, waiting for just the right moment to emerge into the light of spring.

I recently came across a passage in the Bible that I had never read before. In the book of Isaiah, God speaks to a man named Cyrus, promising him that he will lead him to a city that was one of the superpowers of the ancient world, and after the battle for the city, Cyrus will find treasures stored in dark places. "I will give you hidden treasures, riches stored in secret places, so that you may know that I am the LORD, the God of Israel, who summons you by name" (Isa 45:3). The tradition during this time period was to hide all the treasures of a nation underground. The belief was that no one would think such precious treasures would be hidden in the darkest and sometimes dirtiest of places. But God reveals that the most precious treasures will indeed be hidden in the darkness.

We have become quite adept at blessing the light. But darkness is the microcosm for the other half of our lives, the night half that God called good alongside day. No matter how black it may seem, darkness is a pathway to the sunrise up ahead. And even when we are staring straight into the inky night, our eyes are watching God.

In the Bible there is a story about a man named Abraham who felt abandoned by God. He and his wife desperately wanted a family, but month after month Sarah wept at the sight of her monthly

---

2   Barbara Brown Taylor, *Learning to Walk in the Dark* (New York: HarperOne, 2014), 58.

cycle. Even into their old age, the couple felt the sting of unrequited parenthood.

That is, until God whispered to Abraham to go outside and count the stars.

I can imagine Abraham telling Sarah what he heard, a message from God saying that their descendants would be as numerous as the stars. I imagine both of them suppressing nervous laughter because it had to be some sort of cruel joke. After all, Sarah was far past childbearing age, and they were both too old and too experienced to believe in something so extravagant. I can imagine Sarah lying on her back in the dew of the evening, gazing into the darkness completely starry-eyed. She starts with one and continues to number each star, contemplating the promise that Abraham laughingly whispered to her earlier in the day. Abraham, unable to sleep because he is too worried that once again his wife will wake to disappointment, tiptoes out into the dark to bring her a blanket. Sarah takes the blanket, and her cold hands touch the warmth of her husband's. He kisses her softly before he heads back into the comfort of the tent. She continues counting if for no other reason than to take her mind off the hoping for something impossible.

But the night sky holds hope for all of us. Including for Sarah, who had at first laughed with incredulity at an unfathomable promise. As her womb swelled with child, the stars became a nightly reminder of the vast things that God can do.

I wonder how often each of us could benefit from a reminder of God's extravagant promises. From a renewed hope that whispers to us through the vastness of the universe, assuring us that darkness is the fertile ground where life is born, and kisses are shared under glimmering stars.

What would it look like if we began to bless the night? Maybe we start with something like this poem by William John Fitzgerald:

"BLACK CAN BE BEAUTIFUL"

O God, black can be beautiful!
Let us be aware of black blessings:
Blessed be the black night that nurtures dreams.
Blessed be the black hole out of which creation sprang.
Blessed be the black cave of imagination that births creativity.
Blessed be dark wombs that cradle us.
Blessed be black loam that produces nourishing food for our
*   bodies.*
Blessed be black jazz that nourishes our souls.
Blessed be black energy that swirls into gracefulness.
Blessed be black coal that heats us.
Blessed be black boiling clouds hurling down lightning and
*   cleansing rain.*
Blessed be even our own darkness, our raw, undeveloped cave of
*   shadows.*
O God, help us to befriend black and not deny its power.
Help us not to cover over the dark with fear but to open to it with
*   your grace*
and to be open to your life within the dark.
May we discover the blessings that lie deep within our holy dark
so that we may freely affirm that
Black is beautiful indeed![3]

Because a cacophony of stars glimmer with tales of hope born in the darkness.

And it is good.

---

3   William John Fitzgerald, *Blessings for the Fast Paced and Cyberspaced: Parables, Reflections and Prayers*, 2nd ed. (Phoenix: Tau Publishing, 2011), 47. Reprinted by permission of the author.

Q & R

1. When do you experience awe in your present life?

2. How did you feel about darkness and night as a child and teenager?

3. Do you have fear of darkness that has crowded out its hidden treasures?

4. Reflect on and share how darkness nourishes and benefits you.

5. Are you curious and open to discovering what treasures are held inside less-known parts of yourself? In the whole constellation of your life experiences?

* * *

CHAPTER 3

Becoming My Mother:
A Reason to Dance

So a couple of things happened recently that I should probably tell you about. The first is that I complimented a woman at the grocery store on the ugly Christmas sweater she was obviously sporting for an ugly-sweater party, only to find out she wasn't heading to any such party. She just thought it was a great holiday sweater. Secondly, when someone asked my daughter what her favorite meal that I make was, she answered, "Cereal." And on top of all this I realized: I have become my mother.

My realization happened in the hallowed halls of our local grocery store. As I was shopping for the usuals, one of the best songs from the nineties came on, and I was compelled to dance in the aisles. My kids were with me and were completely mortified. But when "Play That Funky Music" comes on, I am going to dance. It might not have been so terrible for my precious and embarrassed children except for the fact that a teenage boy, who was stocking shelves, saw my amazing dance moves, grabbed my hand, and proceeded to spin me around the juice aisle. Bless his heart. It was like a scene out of *Ferris Bueller's Day Off*—but my kids are too young to understand what that means, and I was too busy dancing to explain it to them.

Vivid memories of my mom dancing through stores to her favorite songs flashed through my mind, and I had to laugh. I actually wear this "I am becoming my mother" badge with honor. I couldn't be prouder to share so many qualities with the best woman I know. But there are still a few elusive qualities of hers that I am working on mastering. Like her ability to turn any meal into a feast and any moment into an experience. This is a woman whose blood type is nurturer and whose love is Niagara Falls—powerful and moving.

She and my dad grew up in the same town and went to high school together, but they didn't date until a few years after. He was wild and wore short shorts to show off his legs. She was outgoing and stylish in handmade outfits that my grandma, her mother, made just for her. She was four months older than my dad, and he never let her forget it. On Christmas Eve he proposed. She accepted. And our family was born.

Chuck, Cindy, Mandy, and Charley.

I can't tell you how many times I have seen and heard our names in this exact order. Written on Christmas cards. Recorded on our answering machine.

Of course, Dad was first, because all our early stories begin with him.

He was impulsive. "Let's get horses," he said to my mom. Being the always-ready-for-adventure type, she agreed.

"Let's remodel a farm house." Again mom was all in.

"Let's move to California."

"Back to New York."

"Back to California."

Always in. My mom is a saint that way.

My dad is the one who took me to my first horseback-riding lesson, the one who taught me to love running, who pushed me in sports. He is the one who told me to do hard things even when I didn't feel like it. He made snow forts and drank too much beer. He was a mixture of confidence and insecurity. He was particular about his clothes being pressed just right. He was deeply bonded to my brother and found immense pride in him and his accomplishments. He was an introverted salesman, a self-made success.

As I became a teenager, our relationship became complicated. He was Irish and stubborn and could tell me he loved me only when he thought I was sleeping. He would come in my room, kiss my forehead, and whisper, "I love you." Sometimes I would still be awake and smile to myself. I was okay with his subtle displays of affection because I knew that it was more than he had ever received from his own dad.

The summer after my freshman year of college, I worked away from home. One weekend in late June, I decided to spend a few days at home. My dad knew that I was coming and had heard from my mom that I needed some hiking boots for work. When I arrived, I was greeted with a box of hiking boots sitting on the counter. Dad had spent the afternoon going from store to store in search of the only pair of boots in San Diego that were my size. This was highly unusual for him. In the midst of the complications of life and youth and family that had risen up between us, this was a peace offering of sorts that spoke more than any words he could say.

That night I wrote him a letter. I said things I felt deep in my gut that he needed to hear. I told him I loved him no matter what. That he was a good man, and even though things were sometimes hard between us, they wouldn't always be. We were both evolving and were sure to get our crap together sometime soon. I shoved the note in his briefcase and fell asleep on the couch.

At 5:30 a.m. when my dad woke up for work, I heard the rustle of his briefcase. The note I had written the night before fell out onto the floor. He picked it up and read it. I heard tears. I pretended I was asleep, because it was too many feelings to process that early in the morning. Then he came to the side of the couch, kissed me on the forehead, and left for the day.

Two weeks later I got a weird midday call from my brother.

"I have really bad news."

Dad had gone out for a run and didn't make it home.

I drove home, but I can't remember getting in the car or the hour-long drive. I found my brother lying on his back on the floor, stunned by grief.

There were no words.

Unable to reach her sooner, I remember how my mom's knees buckled when we told her.

Cindy, Mandy, and Charley.

The next year felt like breathing under water. The grief was almost too much to bear, and experiencing any semblance of normal life seemed impossible. Life without my dad felt foreign, and I realized that the future would have to be navigated in ways I had never anticipated. Like having to plan a wedding without him.

Two months before my dad died, I started dating Joe. Dad met Joe twice. Half a year later, Joe and I decided that we wanted to make this a forever thing. He proposed, and we were tasked with planning a wedding and grieving at the same time. It seemed strange to talk about a wedding so soon after a funeral. My life was starting with Joe as I was simultaneously dealing with the end of a life with my dad, and it was so bittersweet that I could barely live it. Everything had more meaning than the one it was originally assigned. For me, planning a wedding meant more than a ceremony and subsequent party to commemorate the beginning of a marriage; it also meant walking down the aisle without my dad. I never imagined I would have to do that. Thankfully, I have the most amazing family and the most amazing friends who are more family than friends. They navigated this whole paradoxical journey with laughter and tears and reminded me that life can be beautiful and tragic at the same time.

After nearly a year full of heartache, and barely beginning to come to terms with the loss of my dad, Joe and I got married. On a beautiful Southern California summer day, we stood in a garden, surrounded by family and friends, and said our vows in front of an amazing arbor that was so beautifully decorated with flowing tulle and cascading flowers that it made me want to cry. Almost everything made me cry. I woke up on my wedding day, feeling out of sorts, and after dealing with a series of frustrations, sat down next to my mom and cried on her shoulder. Poor Joe was probably nervous about what he was committing to. But then the music began to play, and my brother looped his arm through mine and walked me down the aisle.

When I saw my mom dancing at my wedding, I thought of all the times I had seen her dancing in our kitchen or the grocery store over the years. I am thankful for a mom who can find a reason to dance no matter what. She has taught me much about resilience. She kept us all afloat, reminding us we would be okay no matter what. I have no words adequate enough to express the depth of who she is and how she mothered us in spite of her own pain.

And I hope I will grow up to be just like her—a dancing light in the darkness, in the kitchen, or in the grocery store—wherever it is needed. Even when I embarrass my kids, I hope they will see a mom who loves like my mom does—and whose resilience in times of darkness holds a candle for us all.

Q & R

1. What parts of your mother's legacy do you want to carry forward?

2. What parts do you hope to leave behind?

3. Who has modeled joy and resilience for you? How do you try to model it?

* * *

CHAPTER 4

Together, we've Got This:
Sister Courage and
Borrowed Light

All three of my babies were born on their due dates.

I like to attribute this to my sense of punctuality, but anyone who knows me well can attest that this isn't the case. In truth, it is probably some cosmic joke by the master comedian himself, because being on time is not my thing. Recipes and rules also are not my thing, which means that I am flying by the seat of my pants most of the time.

This mindset spills over all areas of my life. I never can muster the ability to have it all together. In fact, I feel like there are a lot of things about being a woman, an adult, and a mom that I should know, but I don't. It's like I missed the day in high school when all the teachers shared highly classified information about how to function as an adult. It probably happened during first-period physics when my friend Drea and I decided our time was better spent listening to R.E.M. in her red Toyota Tercel.

Most of the time I can fake my way through life, convincing strangers that I am a fully functioning adult. That is, until a situation arises that I should be able to maneuver with ease, and I realize I have no idea what I am doing. Like unclogging a toilet or cooking a steak. Those things are hard to fake.

Here are a few other parts of adult life that challenge me:

Domestic Parts. I never have the right kitchen tools. My mother-in-law has come to my house on numerous occasions and been appalled that I didn't have a proper potato peeler or that I am missing the ¾ measuring cup. (I am a firm believer that estimation is a proper cooking technique. Besides, why do you need a ¾ measuring cup? Can't you just fill the one cup three-quarters full?) I am also unable to keep my sink clean or scrub toilets on a regular basis. I cannot for the life of me figure out how real adults have clean bathrooms every day.

Lady Parts. How is it that I can be thirty-six years old and still have no idea when my period is going to start? And what is the deal with Softcups? How could I be so uneducated about the newest in period paraphernalia? Not to mention that for the life of me I cannot find a bra that actually fits. I mean seriously, after nursing three babies, I have resorted to buying bras in the kids' section of Target. Nothing says I have this woman thing nailed down quite like bubblegum-pink bras with the word "sassy" printed on them.

Friend Parts. I try really hard to be a great friend, but sometimes I am mystified by adults who can plan dinner parties and manage to look fantastic, while they mingle with every guest for just the right amount of time. Cut to me: I forget to text people back. I have small, undetectable panic attacks when someone calls because I am secretly terrified of awkward phone conversations. On the other hand, I am an awesome gift giver . . . but will most likely give it to you weeks after your birthday.

Mom Parts. Twelve years into this mom gig and I wish I could tell you that I have it mastered, but I don't. I compare myself with other moms and feel bad for my kids that I don't cut their sandwiches into butterfly shapes or make them pancakes every morning. Last year I sent my daughter to school dressed for pajama day, only to find out that pajama day was the following day. Not to mention that there was one month where we frequented Urgent Care four times in four weeks for two sets of stitches (head and chin), one broken arm (aggressive capture-the-flag injury), and one concussion (playground fail). Try explaining that to your pediatrician.

But here is the rest of the truth: I am really good at snuggling. I make amazing hot chocolate, and I will do cartwheels in the front yard for hours. I don't do chore charts, and my little tribe isn't perfectly behaved, but we love each other like crazy. And my one saving grace, the thing that keeps my head above water in the mom department, and for that matter, in every department in my life, are my friends. Especially the ones who say, "Me too." Friends who assure me that hiding in the bathroom to eat the last brownie without having to share is something we've all done. And two things I know for sure about being an adult friend: showing up is the most important thing you can do for someone, and taking your friend's kids for a night will endear you to her forever.

Could it be that the greatest myth of adulthood is that we should be able to do everything on our own? I think that if we can do this thing together, I just might have a chance.

For Christmas this year, my husband Joe and I and the kids went to San Diego to spend the holidays with my family. On Christmas Eve, we went to church where I grew up, and where my mom still goes. It is always like a homecoming of sorts; you never know who is going to be in town that particular year. This year I was surprised to see my friend Jenny, whom I have known since junior high school. Her family no longer lives in town, so I was surprised and especially glad to see her. She came up from behind me and hugged me, and without even seeing her face I knew who it was. I recognized her hug—a hug I had been the recipient of at least a million times over the years. And even though I hadn't seen her for a few years, I still knew her hug.

After we caught up briefly and then sat down for the service,

I thought about other hugs that are familiar. My mom's hugs smell like L'Air du Temps perfume and feel like home. My Ellie snuggles her head into my stomach when she hugs me; one friend kisses me on the cheek whenever we hug good-bye. It is in this closeness that we really experience one another. It is the kind of closeness cultivated over time that closes the gaps when we need to be far from one another for prolonged periods, because we have fortified one another with our presence.

We have a term in our family called "Sister Courage." It means, "I need you to come with me. I need you by my side." It is an expression that my two little girls use with one another when they need someone to fortify them. When they don't feel like they can proceed alone.

I think at various points in our lives we all need Sister Courage. We need another woman to simply stand next to us, to show up and fortify us with her presence. To hug us and remind us that together, we've got this.

My mom has a best friend who we call Uncle Jodi. (Yes, she is a woman, and yes, we call her Uncle. We also call her Jigga, but that is a whole other story that should only be shared over too much wine.) Over the years, Mom and Uncle Jodi have walked beside one another through more light and darkness than either of them could have imagined when they first met. During high school, my brother lived with Jodi and her saint of a husband, Tom, when my parents moved out of state during his senior year. When my dad died, Jodi invited my mom to live at their house for over a year while she picked up the pieces of her life. Jodi's house is the one I would go to when I needed a place to crash for long weekends during college. She cares for my mom's children as her own.

My mom shows up for Jodi, too. Whenever Jodi is having a party, my mom is her wingwoman, helping her decorate and cook. They celebrate their birthday weekends together, floating in the pool. My mom cries with Jodi when hard and scary things happen in the lives of Jodi's kids. And we have all come to feel that we are family, because Mom and Uncle Jodi insist it is so. The way they have given one another courage just by showing up consistently inspires me to gather my people close. To be honest, even when it's dark. To accept help, even when it's embarrassing. And to never take myself too seriously. Both Mom and Jodi are masterful at all this.

My husband was in Ecuador last summer, visiting our kids we sponsor through Compassion International. While he was there, he was able to visit a part of the country where the people live in extreme poverty. He saw all the amazing things the Compassion center was doing there, like providing kids with two meals a day for four days out of the week. For some of them, these are the only meals they get.

While he was visiting, Joe had the privilege of participating in the daily working of the center, including passing out food to the kids. He called me that night to tell me how he had started at one end of the table, and as he passed a plate over some kids in the middle of the table to reach those at the very end, a little girl about nine years old grabbed the plate and wouldn't let go. He was surprised at how persistent she was being and tried to explain to her that it was for another child, and he would bring hers out shortly. But she wouldn't let go, so he loosened his grip. He was even more surprised when, instead of taking the plate for herself, she turned and gave it to her little sister, who was sitting next to her. Her desperation was on behalf of this little one, who had the hungriest eyes you have ever seen. The older sister was determined that her little sister was going to eat.

Sister Courage means making sure the people around us are fed.

About a year ago I was reading the Mother's Day issue of *Vogue* magazine, which featured an excerpt from Hillary Clinton's memoir *Hard Choices*. If we can all call a truce on our views about her politics, then we can appreciate the part of the excerpt that is intensely important. Hillary shares how her mother's childhood was marked by abandonment and trauma, then tells about a time when she realized how resilient her mom was. Hillary shared:

> When I got old enough to understand all this, I asked my mother how she survived abuse and abandonment without becoming embittered and emotionally stunted. How did she emerge from this lonely early life as such a loving and levelheaded woman? I'll never forget how she replied. "At critical points in my life somebody showed me kindness," she said. Sometimes it would seem so small, but it would mean so much—the teacher in elementary school who noticed that she never had money to buy milk, so every day would buy two cartons of milk and then say, "Dorothy, I can't drink this other carton of milk. Would you like it?" Or the woman who hired her as a nanny and insisted that she go to high school. One day she noticed that Mom had only one blouse that she washed every day. "Dorothy, I can't fit into this blouse anymore and I'd hate to throw it away. Would you like it?" she said.[1]

Sister Courage notices when someone needs help and offers them dignity.

Last week, I met a friend for coffee. For as long as I have known her, she has been stylish and beautiful and comfortable in her own skin, all things I want to be. She is confident and at ease, while I tend to second guess my every thought. And I have been jealous of her through the years. Lately, however, my jealousy has turned into admiration. I realized that I had been envious because she gave herself permission that I didn't give myself. She was comfortable fanning her spark into a flame, while I tried to hide mine. I decided

---

1   "An Exclusive Excerpt from Hillary Clinton's Upcoming Book, *Hard Choices*," *Vogue*, n.d., http://www.vogue.com/865125/hillary-clinton-book-hard-choices/.

that instead of feeling insecure around her, I could learn something about being more myself.

Sister Courage means gaining the freedom to be ourselves because we have seen others owning themselves.

The brilliant Albert Schweitzer said, "At times our own light goes out and is rekindled by a spark from another person. Each of us has cause to think with deep gratitude of those who have lighted the flame within us."[2]

That is the soul of Sister Courage. It offers a spark in order to rekindle the flame in the sisters all around us.

Sister Courage says, "We are family, and together, we've got this."

Q & R

1. Which parts of adulthood have come naturally to you? Which have you struggled with?

2. Who inspires you to own who you are and fans your spark into a flame?

3. Who in your life can you help to feed and dignify?

4. What can you do to inspire others to be more and more of who they were created to be?

* * *

---

2   Albert Schweitzer, *Thoughts for Our Times* (Mount Vernon, NY: Peter Pauper Press, 1975), 16.

CHAPTER 5

Dear Fifteen:
Permission to Sit
with Our Pain

Kristen and I were neighbors for three years and friends for twenty years before that. We met in junior high when we both had braces and feathered bangs. She is thoughtful and artistic and a great cook. I am not a good cook. We dated the same boy. She stole him from me in tenth grade. I forgive her.

Not long ago, my family went to visit her and her husband Si in San Diego where Kristen and I grew up, and she invited us over for dinner. I sat at the butcher-block counter in the center of their kitchen, gaggles of kids running in and out, husbands coaching each other on business ventures, and I couldn't help but remember how at fifteen Kristen and I spent long nights wondering what our lives were going to look like.

I wish I could send a postcard to our fifteen-year-old selves with a handwritten love note like this:

Dear Kristen and Mandy . . . I know right now it's all about Gap overalls and the latest episode of Saved by the Bell. *But sometime in the not-so-far-off future, you'll be having dinner and talking about nursing babies, how you get to do work you love, college funds, how sleeping is the new drinking, and all the funny things your kids say. I know it sounds crazy, but you will have seven babies between you, and you will pick each*

other's kids up from school. You will get your hearts broken. It will suck.
But the men each of you choose to spend life with will be more than worth
it. So keep singing show tunes and eating ice cream for breakfast, because
your lives turn out pretty great. Also, Kristen, you'll get boobs eventually,
so stop worrying about it. Mandy . . . not so much. But stop worrying
about it anyway.

Sitting at Kristen's counter that night made me take notice of all the beautiful things we had swirling around us in that kitchen, twenty years after we worried they never would. I wish I could have reassured our teenage selves that all these good things were heading our way. But the truth is, I would have also had to share that there would be a lot of hard and sad things in between then and now.

Between the years of fifteen and thirty-six, Kristen's parents divorced. My dad died. She endured a relationship that was abusive. I struggled with debilitating depression. But what I believe both of us would say is that it is all good. That the sorrow and pain are as much a part of the process as the lovemaking and celebrations.

The fact that we are human means uncomfortable feelings will be a part of our experience here. Between Kristen and me, we have birthed seven babies into the world. Kris is the kind of girl who pushed her babies out without any pain medication. I asked for epidurals as soon as I walked in the door. Well, maybe not as soon as I walked in the door. With each baby I convinced myself that I would go au natural, and each time I succumbed to pain relief after laboring for a few hours.

Each time our babies were pushing their way toward their first breath, the nurses would remind us to work with the pain. This is the first time I really experienced how productive pain can be. When laboring, the best way to navigate the pain is to sit with it. To move with it and let it do its job. Instead of fighting against it, the most productive posture is surrender. You can't get to the other side without it.

And the other side? Is breathtakingly beautiful.

I wish I had learned this lesson earlier, because for most of my life I have been running from pain. Including during labor. It always seemed to me that pain, sorrow, and heartache were feelings to avoid at any cost. This meant I was constantly doing mental gymnastics to pretend all those feelings weren't there.

That is, until I couldn't pretend any longer.

When my dad died unexpectedly my sophomore year of college, my world came crashing down. On top of mourning my dad and worrying about my mom, I had a bit of a spiritual crisis. Life didn't make any sense, and I became undone with anxiety. My body, picking up on my extreme emotional duress, started to exhibit physical symptoms that reflected my inner struggle. I went to the hospital twice with panic attacks that terrified me. I was physically exhausted and emotionally unraveled.

I come from a long line of the suck-it-up sort. We are masterful at making the best of a situation. This is a really helpful quality to have in life; that is, until darkness comes like a tidal wave, and there are no boats to rescue you. When my dad died, the grief and pain and worry were too real, and all my efforts to pretend they weren't there led me straight into a season of darkness I couldn't push my way through. I had to sit with it and face it head on.

Have you ever been given permission to sit with your pain? Maybe instead of trying to outrun the pain, you need to sit with it for a while. To look it in the eye and acknowledge it is there. Is it possible your pain is waiting to be seen, and that only then can it pass?

I am learning that the best way to navigate pain is to sit with it, to move with it, and to let it do its work. Instead of fighting against it, sometimes the most productive posture is surrender. Too often we spend our time trying to be one step ahead, staying so busy we don't ever have to admit to what our insides are feeling. That's why we drink and eat and cheat and shop and hit and gossip and hurt each other. Because we cannot handle our difficult feelings. Because we cannot trust pain as a teacher. We are like caterpillars who quit right before we'd become butterflies.

What if we stopped running from pain and decided to sit still and to trust the process?

About six months after my dad died, I met my mom for dinner at a mall that was halfway between her work and my college. We sat in the food court and ate chow mein with chopsticks. Having my mom there, listening to my fears and sorrow, freed me to spill my guts. I told her about how scared I was, how out of control life felt, and I bawled my eyes out, surrounded by all sorts of shoppers looking for a deal. As my tears kept coming, she grabbed my hand and practically picked me up and sat me on her lap, which made me cry even harder. In a moment of maternal instinct, all she could think to do was hold me close like she had so many years previously. She wrapped her arms around me and rocked my nineteen-year-old frame, while whispering prayers into my ear and the ear of God.

At that moment, I lost any sense of self-consciousness that my mom was holding me on her lap in such a public place, because I needed someone to sit with me in my grief. To literally feel with her body the weight of pain that I was carrying. My mom didn't try to fix anything that day. She didn't offer any advice. Instead, she held me and hugged me until I had cried all my tears. She sat with me and shared in my sadness.

Not only do we give ourselves a gift when we make space to sit with our pain, but we can also offer that gift to one another. Pain is part of being human. A delicate part that interlaces with the holy and allows us to empathize with the hurting places in the world and in our own hearts.

As my kids have gotten older, I have been giving this permission to them. Refraining from trying to rush in and make all their feelings go away so they will never feel uncomfortable. Perhaps giving our kids permission to feel their pain means that, when they get their feelings hurt or feel sad about breaking a toy, we choose to sit with them in their sorrow instead of rushing in to distract them from their feelings or replace their broken toy. Or maybe it means simply listening to them when they come home from school, wounded by mean words from a friend. Could it be that the best way to show up for our kids and our friends who are deeply enmeshed in sorrow is to simply sit and share in it with them? Without offering words that act as pathetic Band-Aids clinging to gaping wounds, perhaps we simply sit and breathe alongside them, allowing our presence to be enough.

Not long ago, I witnessed a moment that took the air out my lungs. Miss Ellie Elizabeth had to endure a ridiculously extensive dental appointment that no five-year-old should have to undergo. Since everyone was out of school for the summer, Joseph (eight) and Charlotte J. (three) had to accompany us to the appointment. After an hour of dental procedures, we left the office with a whimpering Ellie, who was beginning to feel the pain as the novocaine and laughing gas wore off. During our twenty-minute drive home, the whimpering became large wet tears that evolved into shrill screams from a little girl who didn't understand why her mouth was hurting so badly. I wanted to throw up. I think one of the most horrific things for a parent is to see a child in pain. It was almost unbearable because there was little I could do for her. It was a waiting game for the pain meds to kick in, and until they did, all I could do was listen and pray the pleading prayers of a mom who desperately wants to make everything all better NOW.

And then it happened. In a small voice, from the seat next to me, Joseph looked back at Ellie and said, "I feel like crying for you." In a moment of helpless empathy, my eight-year-old boy cried for his sister. And then, seeing his gesture, I cried. We all cried together, sharing in the suffering of our Ellie.

Within a few minutes, we were home. Ellie was asleep, and Joseph was playing Legos. But for one small moment, Joseph shared his sister's pain and taught his mom that sometimes, even though we don't have the words to make things better, we can make a moment better by sitting, feeling, and sharing a good cry.

We live in a culture that idolizes personal happiness. We are told to pursue self-improvement at any cost. We are supposed to be so content, so fulfilled and happy all the time—and if we aren't perpetually blissed out we are somehow failing. That narrative isn't useful for any of us. Because pain doesn't mean we are doing life wrong. It just means we are doing life.

Adversity is what shapes us into richly complex souls who have ridden the tidal wave of pain and have lived to tell the tales. What Kristen and I have learned over the years is that there is a tremendous amount of light in the darkness.

Did you know that God tells us he dwells in darkness? In the book of 1 Kings we read, "It came to pass, when the priests had come out of the holy place, that the cloud filled Yahweh's house, so that the priests could not stand to minister by reason of the cloud; for Yahweh's glory filled Yahweh's house. Then Solomon said, 'Yahweh has said that he would dwell in the thick darkness. I have surely built you a house of habitation, a place for you to dwell in forever'" (1 Kgs 8:10–13 WEB).

God says he will dwell in the darkness of a thick cloud. In Hebrew, they have a special word for this darkness. The word is *araphel* and means a thick, dark cloud. We read that this dark cloud is a sign of God's mercy, because humans are not equipped to survive direct contact with the Holy One. Therefore, it is only through this darkness, where his presence is obscured, that we can experience God. There are treasures hidden in the dark. And even when we are staring straight into the darkness, our eyes are watching God.

So if you are in a season where you need to sit with some pain, remember that sometimes the light is coming and sometimes it is going. Here is the honest truth, friends. Sometimes we need to go talk to someone, sometimes we need to go on meds to help our bodies regulate, and other times we just need to sit with our darkness, look it in the eye, and wait. Because the light ebbs and flows, and there is nothing capricious about this process, since it happens on a regular basis. Is it dark out tonight? Fear not; there are hidden treasures to be found. So find comfort in your discomfort. Let your pain flow deeply in and deeply out. Sit with it, move with it, and let it do its work.

And when we do, we might just find that our fifteen-year-old selves have nothing to worry about.

Q & R

1. Do you think it's possible to hold joy and suffering in tension?

2. Have you ever been given permission to sit with your pain? Can you think of a time when you saw pain in your life be productive, such as the pain of childbirth?

3. What is your most automatic response to pain? Avoid? Minimize? Accept?

4. In what ways have the difficult times in your life made you deeper, more compassionate, or more complex?

* * *

CHAPTER 6

He Had Me at "Ugh":
Joe, Marriage, and
Creating a Legacy

The day we met, Joe almost fell off a cliff. It was a beautiful day in San Diego, and my friend Sarah and I decided that a run along the coast seemed like a great way to spend a Saturday morning. So we left our dorm and headed for the cliffs overlooking the Pacific. The sun was out for the first time in a few days, and the trail along the cliffs was crowded with joggers, who all had the same idea we did.

We were a mile or two into our run when I noticed this cute guy running toward us. I had seen him around campus, but never officially met him. He had his shirt off, which I judged him for—but also enjoyed. Who did this guy think he was, all buff and glistening? I was sure he was a jerk, because the really hot guys sometimes are (or so I believed in college).

As we continued to run toward one another, he got about ten feet in front of us, made eye contact with me, and then tripped. "UGH!" was the first sound I ever heard him utter. He nearly fell off the cliff next to us. It all happened so fast, and he hopped up so quickly, there was no time to ask if he was okay. He kept on running, and so did we, in different directions.

As soon as we were far enough away that he couldn't hear, Sarah said very matter-of-factly, "He totally likes you."

A few months later, he called me out of the blue and left a message with a super-cheesy pickup line. I decided to go on a date with him in spite of said pickup line.

First dates always made my palms sweat. As I waited for Joe to pick me up for the first time, I was shooting up silent prayers that he wouldn't grab my hand, because my nerves would be exposed. I wanted to play it like I was super cool and this was no big deal. His white, two-door Honda pulled into the parking lot. He greeted me with a hug (I owe you one, almighty God of love) and flowers he had picked from the side of the road. His smile was confident, but his eyes gave him away: he was just as nervous as I was.

We made small talk as my friends sized him up and made sure he was the real deal. Waving goodbye to all my ladies, we walked to his car. He opened the door, I climbed in, and we drove off for a ferry ride across the harbor. We walked to Coronado Beach and talked for hours. On our walk back, it poured buckets, but we didn't even notice.

He still tells people that he fell for me the moment he saw me. Literally.

He had me at "ugh."

Joe is a guy who wears patience like a tailored suit. He is charismatic but doesn't know it and makes you feel like you are his best friend within minutes of meeting him. This also means that everyone who meets him loves him, because he is gifted like that. It is a quality that is elusive to me. I have always envied him for an attribute I am not even sure he knows he has. He inspires me, and I am grateful to spend my days with him.

And we have spent a lot of days together. Not all of them have been amazing, mostly because I am emotional and pouty sometimes. In fact, last night I was distracted because Joe and I had one of those long "things feel off between us right now—how do we fix it" conversations. He had been traveling a lot, which means I might have been throwing a little pity party for myself, because I had had full-time parenting duty with two kids who had the stomach flu. I think I also had a touch of PMS. My bad attitude may or may not have contributed to the poor guy missing out on the warm welcome home he anticipated.

When Joe and I first met, we were both different versions of ourselves: the dating versions. We were always showered and thoughtful. I wore makeup to sleep, and he wrote me poetry. But what I've come to realize over time is that the beginning only counts for so much. It is the middle where you really fall in love. Not in the honeymoon kind of lusty love we felt at the start, but in the beautiful, I-really-know-you kind of way. When this happens, it is a profound experience because you know the other person has seen your best and worst and loves you in spite of it.

In the beginning, I thought I had married someone who made me happy, but all these years later I realize I actually found someone who makes me better: a man who will put up with my unsavory parts, up until they make me a lesser version of myself. Then he swoops in with truth and help that sometimes doesn't feel like help, but is. No one has mirrored back to me my flaws like my husband has, and no one has been as tender in tolerating them, either. Our marriage is at its best when we are helping each other become better versions of ourselves without sacrificing the parts of ourselves that make us uniquely great. We are collaborating on a legacy that will shape our family for generations to come.

Often I lay in bed at night, Joe to my right, and listen to the slow gentle rhythm of his breathing. I think of all the nights we have laid next to one another. Some of those nights were filled with passion, other nights we have had one or three kids snuggled in between us. There have been times when I cried myself to sleep, and he snuggled up to me, patiently letting me feel all my feelings. This man and I have shared as much sunlight and moonlight as two people can share. And through it all, the love keeps getting brighter.

This kind of love is hard to quantify because it takes on various manifestations and meanings. Add the concept of God into the mix, and it gets even more complex. I have always understood that God is loving, but it didn't always feel that way. If I am completely honest, I thought God's love was a nice idea, but I could never internalize it. Then I came across imagery of God as a bridegroom. A spouse. And I started to think about my relationship with my husband. Joe is the person who knows everything about me. We share a bed; we made a family; we are intimate on a level I don't experience with anyone else. He gets me. I am my most vulnerable, my most naked, my most trusting with him. I care so deeply about him as an individual that I do everything in my power to help him live his most passionate life, and he does the same for me.

Interestingly, this is how God wants to reveal himself to us, with the intimacy of a spouse. God uses imagery to show us that he is all the things that make a relationship intimate. He wants to hold our gaze in the same way we are mesmerized by staring into a fire or a lover's eyes. The energy around lovers is infused with their longings and delight. They look toward one another for reassurance when life gets shaky. They give themselves fully to one another, and they make room for mistakes. God does, too.

There is a long-held tradition in at least one faith practice of blurring the distinction between human and divine love. When Hindus greet each other, they bow and say, "Namaste," which means, "I recognize God in you." I recognize God, the very essence of love itself, because I have seen him in Joe. In response, all the love I give to the people with whom I spend my days is a unique manifestation of the divine love God makes available to all of us. We help one another know God by how well we love each other. And that love is our legacy.

Q & R

1. Reflect on the ways you have seen the divine reflected in your spouse, children, family, or friends.

2. What legacy are you striving to create for your children?

3. What intentional steps are you taking to create that legacy?

* * *

CHAPTER 7

In the Belly of the Holy One:
Birthing a New Concept of God

Anytime a baby is born in my circle of friends, there is a day, typically a week or so after mom and baby have come home, when all the friends show up at the new mom's house to hear her birthing story. There isn't a plan; we have never discussed why this happens. But without fail we all feel like we need to be together. So we show up.

As we sit around taking turns holding the baby, we listen attentively while our friend, a warrior woman who was opened up to the world just days ago, regales us with her battle stories. Each time this happens, I am astounded by the details we share with one another. They are gory and intimate—because birthing is not sweet and sanitary. It is earthy and guttural and bloody. Nothing is held back. The process of bringing new life into the world has to be shared and processed together.

After hearing all the details and asking all the questions, we tend to our friend. We ask if she has slept, we wash her dishes and make her favorite tea. We bring meals and pick up her kids. Pushing life from your body feels deeply satisfying and also deeply terrifying. So we make space for her to process, because laboring is something that can be fully understood only by women who have experienced it themselves.

When I was laboring with each of my kids, I remember thinking about the women all over the world who were laboring with me that day. Women who were just as scared as I was. Sisters who didn't have access to pain medication or to a comfortable bed. I imagined women in shanty towns whose only medical intervention was their mother and sisters who had experienced labor themselves. While I had no idea who they were, the women who labored with me that day became a ray of light reminding me I wasn't alone.

While I could rely on the women around me to share in all the uniquely feminine experiences of birth, I began to have an issue with God when it came to all this laboring. This uniquely female experience felt so separate from him. Probably this is because I have grown up in a culture that has assigned God a male pronoun. Also, it is because we read in the beginning of God's story that pain in childbirth is because of a curse brought on by a woman who was tempted by knowledge. Being both a woman who is tempted by knowledge and also of childbearing age, these details cast a shadow on my being able to make peace with my feminine reality and a masculine understanding of God. I had a deep desire to find a relationship between God and the deep feminine birthing energies that were radiating from my core.

A woman once told me her favorite thing about Jesus was his mom, and for a long time, Mary was the closest I could get to divine femininity. Mary was a female whose body worked on a natural lunar cycle. She had experienced growing and birthing life, and she was considered blessed. The problem for me was that it seemed like the Catholics already had dibs on her, and I had no frame of reference on how to incorporate her into my daily spiritual life. In light of that reality, how was I to process what holy femininity looked like?

Of course, I turned where I always do in these kinds of situations: straight to books. I poured through texts about language and the nature of God, and then I figured a good place to look might be the book that is considered God-breathed. So I studied the Bible for truths that would help me find balance between the nature of God as masculine and feminine.

What I read opened a door and cracked a light in the darkness for me. I began to realize that I had been introduced to only one archetype of God. My lack of knowledge about the imagery God uses to explain himself was a big part of my problem. I learned that along with all the masculine attributes, there are many feminine images that God uses to describe himself. The Holy Spirit is at times referred to as feminine energy. In Hosea, God is likened to a fierce mother bear protecting her cubs. Continue reading, and God takes on the image of a mother hen, a nursing mother, a woman looking for a lost coin, and last but not least, a laboring mother.

In Isaiah 42, God labors for the ones he loves, saying:

> For a long time I have kept silent, I have been quiet and held myself back. But now, like a woman in childbirth, I cry out, I gasp and pant. . . . I will turn rivers into islands and dry up the pools. I will lead the blind by ways they have not known, along unfamiliar paths I will guide them; I will turn the darkness into light before them and make the rough places smooth. These are the things I will do; I will not forsake them. (Isa 42:14–16)

These are the cries of a laboring God: feminine, powerful, and bursting with the hope of new life.

Julian of Norwich understood this divine laboring and explained it by saying that we are born from the very womb of the divine. This is why she regularly referred to God as both Father and Mother. She believed that all of life was embryonic, "in the belly," of the Holy One. That which has never been before is birthed from deep within. Love results in pregnant hope, labor brings about new life. This means that God identifies with the blood and grit and gore of birthing. And the very real experience of deepest pain and deepest joy mixed so thoroughly it is hard to tell where one begins and the other ends . . . God gets that, too.

Our universe is a miscellany of polarities, light and dark, hope and despair, night and day, masculine and feminine, and much of our lives is spent trying to find a healthy balance of both. That is why this imagery of God helps me understand the masculine God I have always known alongside my own feminine birthing energy that is a reflection of a part of God I am unearthing. This process of discovery has revealed new attributes of God that affirm that the feminine is holy and good and deeply needed. I am reminded that women are uniquely made to birth light and life into the world, and our feminine gifts are a direct reflection of the nature of God.

I believe that our bodies are good, more so than we have ever imagined. Not only are they good, but I believe that God communicates to us through our bodies. Rather than being an inconvenience, what if we acknowledged that from the depths of our being, God is birthing new life into our world? From the depth of our unknown places, new life, new creativity, and new hope are bleeding out from our bodies and souls. We are the creative catalyst of God's feminine attributes.

This is why I believe that instead of a curse, we are actually blessed—all of us who labor. This is because a truer sense of God's nature reveals to all of us women that we are not "other." We are understood by God. We are made in his masculine and feminine image. Maybe all of it, the pain and pushing and miraculous ending, are a glimpse into something bigger that only we get a sneak peek into, because we labor like the Holy One.

Q & R

1. What do you think about this biblical image of God as a mother? What do you think it tells us about who he is?

2. Where else in your life besides childbirth/adoption have you experienced pain, pushing, and a miracle ending?

* * *

CHAPTER 8

Confidence over Conformity:
Reclaiming Our Birthrights

Sometimes we just need to tell the truth and to make some unknowns known.

I've spent a whole lot of my life trying to be different than I am at my core. Trying to be less of everything. Less sensitive. Less of my cussy-mouth self. Less sentimental. Less me. Trying to make it appear like I have everything in balance. Dulling my creativity to stay inside the lines. I just wanted to be acceptable. Presentable. I wanted to fit in. Similar to the moon, part of me was always hidden away.

I am pretty sure it started in high school. My family had just moved to a new town, and I wanted to fit in. But the first acquaintance I met said things to me like, "You dress weird; you think too much; you laugh too loudly." My soul felt sunburned, like I had been overexposed, and all I wanted was to be healed from all this feeling and being. I didn't want to stand out or have my differences noticed. So I talked myself into believing I had to make myself smaller. And I shrank, suffering from a year-long battle with an eating disorder as a result of needing to *literally* make myself less. I was afraid to fill my space in this world.

But I am not okay with that kind of thinking anymore.

I don't know whether it is the accumulation of years or hearing family friends share about my dad at his funeral that is saving me in this department. My dad was a passionate person. He coached football and would get so worked up on the sidelines that his face would become red, and he would yell or cheer at the top of his lungs. You couldn't ignore him. And at his funeral, one person after another got up to share about how he influenced them, about how they appreciated his passion, and how it was his "too much" they loved most about him.

It was like smelling salts to me. It woke me up to the fact that conformity is boring. It is uniqueness that is compelling. We fall in love with each other's rough edges. Our "too much" makes us endearing.

For me, giving myself permission to be too much means that I show up in big ways. I bring a gift when it isn't expected; I rewrite a song for a friend's fortieth birthday and force my husband to perform it with me; I go out of my way to let people know how much I love them; I give myself permission to feel and to be silly. This can be embarrassing for my kids. They question why I need to hug everyone I meet, or why I always get picked out of a crowd to go up on stage. My husband wonders why I have to put so much extra effort into picking out the perfect gift and maybe gets a little frustrated when I insist on including him in my shenanigans. Without fail, though, we will be driving home, and he will acknowledge that things are better when I go big.

Giving ourselves permission to be all of who we are doesn't mean that we can spew our emotions all over everyone else. It doesn't mean we can bulldoze other people or intentionally make them uncomfortable. What it does mean is that we are free from overanalyzing our every move. We get to live in the truth that our uniqueness is a gift to the world. Our light is meant to be lived, to be shared. Because we all have an inner fire, a uniqueness that burns hot under our skin, and as we navigate life we choose to either fan or to extinguish that flame.

I love this quote from the movie *Little Women*:

> **Jo March:** I find it poor logic to say that because women are good, women should vote. Men do not vote because they are good; they vote because they are male, and women should vote, not because we are angels and men are animals, but because we are human beings and citizens of this country.
>
> **Mr. Mayer:** You should have been a lawyer, Miss March.
>
> **Jo March:** I should have been a great many things, Mr. Mayer.[1]

"A great many things" makes sense to me.

I long to live on a farm with chickens and horses and a huge garden that grows everything we need to live. I also love the hustle of city life. On weekends I almost never wear makeup, and bell bottoms and moccasins are my go-to getup. At work on Monday, I can sport a pencil skirt and collared white blouse with the best of them. I love to travel, but having roots feels deeply nourishing. I am pretty sure I will need to live a thousand lifetimes to be all the things I am.

The world doesn't need more people hiding the truth of who they really are beneath uniforms of conformity. What it needs is more people who are brave enough to come out of hiding in order to be their great many things. Instead of feeling like we need to choose one thing, we are free to explore all of ourselves without fear of being too much or too weird. We are invited to fan our flame, because we no longer feel constrained by the narratives that try to define us.

---

1   "Little Women (1994): Quotes," *IMDb*, http://www.imdb.com/title/tt0110367/quotes.

Blogger and writer Erin Loechner puts it brilliantly when she says:

> I think of this whenever I get into a tizzy about how I'm straddling my own fence; when I'm falsely believing that I need to pick one or the other. We cannot have it all, because we're already all of it. We are mothers and daughters, and we can be teachers and wives and really bad cooks that sometimes go to yoga but mostly just wear yoga pants. We can be foodies who frequent Chick-fil-A, and we can be skincare experts who battle breakouts. We can be stylists in sweat pants and cobblers in bare feet. We can be mothers who emanate serenity and peace and yet, we might still cry in a heap over spilled rice . . . People are unbelievable. They are swirly mixes, like constellations, like carousels.[2]

We are all swirling constellations, and we get to create a life that reflects a great many things.

The only rule is we don't get to compare it to anyone else's.

My friend Jared Mackey is a shaman disguised as a cigarette-smoking, cocktail-mixing pastor at a community called TNL. I heard him talking once about a unique museum we have in Denver. It houses all of Clyfford Still's art. Every single piece. The story is that he chose five cities that he offered to gift his entire life's work to if they agreed to build a museum that would hold only his work. Denver was the city that agreed. Now, just a block down from the Denver Art Museum is the Clyfford Still Museum, an entire building devoted to the lifetime achievements of one individual. It feels like a pretty gutsy move by Clyfford Still to suggest that his works deserve a dedicated space. I mean, even the Picassos and Monets are spread throughout the world for everyone's appreciation. Some

---

2 Kelle Hampton, "Erin Loechner on Style and Substance: Woman Crush Wednesday," *Enjoying the Small Things*, 27 May 2015, http://kellehampton.com/2015/05/erin-loechner-on -style-and-substance-woman-crush-wednesday.html#sthash.vcH8xcim.dpuf.

people view his demands as megalomania, but I think that Clyfford Still may be on to something.

When you visit the museum, you are able to spiral through the exhibit, starting with his earliest works, then through the middle years, and culminating with his final four pieces. Four simple canvases with little blotches of paint on them. Walking through the museum, it is as if you can *feel* the narrative of his life, starting as a young painter who was drawn to realism and ending with a bent toward abstract expressionism. His art shows the progressive evolution of a lifetime that can easily be appreciated when his collection is viewed as a whole.

Any idea why Clyfford Still wanted his entire art collection to be housed by itself? The reason is he believed that no artist should compare his art to another artist's. He said that when we put our work on display next to another's, our instinct is to compare one to the other, and that is not good for the soul. We are most able to appreciate progress and beauty when we are more concerned with measuring our own rather than analyzing everyone else's.

I compare myself to other women more often than I am comfortable admitting. I try to be excited for other people when they land a huge promotion or look stunning in an outfit. But the truth is, a lot of the time I just feel envious. That is until a friend of mine reframed this conversation for me. She said that envy is admiration holding its breath. I really love that idea. Like, a lot. She also said we feel envious when we notice others doing what we are created to do. Noticing what makes our feelings of envy flair up can be a glimpse into our destiny.

Do you have a sense that you were created to do something? The Bible talks a lot about birthright. It is the idea that we have inherent inclinations and abilities woven into our souls from the beginning of time. Most often these abilities show up when we are young. Loving to paint or banging on a piano, taking cardboard boxes and making them into fantastical creations, being a leader on the playground, or standing up to bullies. Too often as adults we forego our birthrights for more predictable or profitable ways to fill our days. Sometimes it starts when we go to school, and our magic gets graded out of us. Other times it is due to financial constraints. But more often than not, we simply forget about these unique talents when life gets demanding. How sad that we forego what is meant to give us more life for things that may pay the bills but leave us feeling like we aren't fulfilling what we were put on earth to do. What if instead of dismissing our childhood dreams as fantasy, we had a healthy awareness of the life we have settled for and the desires that still call us? In this sense, envy can be the messenger of our unlived life, calling us to attention and action.

How do we reclaim our birthrights? I am pretty sure it starts with remembering and words. I was looking through a shoebox of photos from my childhood a few months ago. I had been visiting my mom and went into her closet to borrow a pair of shoes. Behind the ironing board, I noticed the box of photos and sat down on the carpet to relive memories. Looking through those photos reminded me who I was. I came home to a part of myself I had long forgotten.

Something my friend Sarah did to rekindle her birthrights is to journal her childhood. She started with her first memory and recorded every memory she could recall. As she wrote, patterns started to emerge. She remembered that she loved to sew, and that her teachers would always compliment her handwriting. Know where that simple exercise led Sarah? At forty, she gradually started cultivating her craft and is now a professional chalk artist working with huge brands on marketing campaigns.

May we all become curious about our birthrights, for they are a light we offer to the world.

May our childhood dreams kindle in our hearts a freedom to journey beyond the old limits of all that has become wearisome.

May we listen to the voice of envy that disturbs us when we have settled for something safe.

May we fan our flame and illuminate the space we occupy.

And may we feel deep satisfaction in being a swirling constellation of a great many things.

Q & R

1. Was confidence or conformity encouraged in your family of origin?

2. When are you most tempted to make yourself small? When do you feel the most permission to go big?

3. Think about what, where, and who fans or extinguishes your flame. Think about your own tendency to fan or extinguish the flames of others. Write about what you notice.

4. What were your childhood interests, proclivities, and dreams?

5. Can you dare to dream about and put into words the inherent inclinations and abilities woven into your soul from the beginning of time?

* * *

CHAPTER 9

Breathing in the Light:
Drawing Inspiration from the People around Us

I really love words. Like, a lot. So you may need to humor me for a few minutes here.

Take the word *breath*. In almost every language, you will find a dual meaning for the word. From Hebrew (*ruakh*) to Latin (*spiritus*), the word for breath is typically the same as the word for spirit.[1]

When we talk about the spirit of something, what we're naming is its ethos, the way it makes us feel, the ideas that are sparked in our minds when we interact with it. Take a song, for example. Certain pieces of music move us in powerful ways, and the word we often use is *inspiring*. We mean that it breathed into us something good, hopeful, true, comforting, healing, or genuine.

I believe the same spirit can be appreciated in the people all around us.

I overheard a conversation yesterday because I am nosy, and the two women were enchanting.

They were sitting on a green velvet couch in the corner of a hotel I was staying at on business. Sitting close, almost knee to

---

1   Rob Bell, "What is the Bible? Part 31: Inspiration," *Rob Bell*, 22 January 2014, http://robbellcom.tumblr.com/post/74194409818/what-is-the-bible-part-31-inspiration.

knee, one had silver gray hair and wore red lipstick; even from fifteen feet away she smelled like Chanel Nº5 perfume. The other was a woman who had bright eyes, a pink nose from holding back tears, and two babes playing at her feet.

As I pretended to check emails on my phone so that I could linger near the couch without distracting them, I overheard these words spoken through the bright red lips of wisdom: "You are going to be a thousand different women in your lifetime; there is no need to worry about what you aren't right now. Soon enough, you will be more than you ever imagined. Just focus on breathing deeply and being inspired."

Breathing deeply felt like a good idea to me at that very moment, since I had been holding my breath trying to make out every word that passed between these two souls sharing a moment in a dark corner of a hotel.

I am always amazed at how inspiration is all around us, swirling between red lips and over babes playing on the floor and into our hearts at exactly the right moment, even if we were eavesdropping to hear it. Usually, when I'm feeling like I don't have anything to offer to the world, it's because I have forgotten how to appreciate the light that dances around me in the form of the people sitting next to me.

A few weeks ago, a friend reminded me of a quote I had heard years ago, something about how to be inspired is to breathe in light. That idea came back to me as I watched these kindreds on the couch remind one another to be inspired. I thought about how, if I had to add to the quote, I would make it not only about inspiration but about being inspired by the light of the people around us. By the ones who smell like Chanel as well as the ones who smell like playdough. In order to appreciate ourselves, sometimes we need to learn to appreciate others by breathing them in. And maybe that is the inspiration we have been gasping for all along.

I have a no-crying-at-work policy, but yesterday I shut my door, crawled under my desk, and bawled my eyes out. The tears began forming earlier in the day when I received a mean email from a woman who told me Jesus hated me because of an article I wrote in MOPS International's *Hello, Dearest* magazine. This was followed by a meeting with a colleague, who informed me in no uncertain terms that she was going back on her word about something that was important to me. When my morning culminated in almost losing a big advertising deal, I decided it was one of those days when the only appropriate response is to crawl under your desk and let warm salty tears roll down your cheeks, uninhibited.

By chance, my friend and coworker Liz called me not long after the crying incident. She sensed that I was barely keeping it together, and without me having to tell her any details, she began to speak words over me that I didn't think I deserved. She reminded me of qualities I had forgotten about myself, and then spoke hope and light into the situations I was worried about. She ended our conversation by telling me a hilarious story about how she went to get a massage, only to find that the masseur was a Jake Gyllenhaal look-alike. She informed him that he was simply too good-looking to massage her. She reassured him that he was probably very good at his job, but she was only interested in having what she describes as "homely looking women" massage her body.

In one short conversation, Liz turned my weeping into tears of laughter. Liz breathes life into my soul. And that is true even when she is breathing through her own darkness. Her marriage is on shaky ground, and she is barely keeping her head above water, but she isn't afraid to e-mail all the difficult details to ask for help, nor has she lost her love of all things quirky and cool. (She regularly sends me updates on her most recent art purchases.) Not only that, but she is willing to drop everything and remind a teary friend that all hope is not lost even though that friend has spent an hour crying under her desk.

I believe that the God who has breathed life into dirt can also breathe new life into people or events that appear to be, at some level, dead. All of us, humble bags of bones and skin, have been inspired by the infinite, eternal creative force of the universe who has breathed into us and everyone around us. This means we are surrounded by infinite potential to be inspired and to come back to life (or emerge from under our desk)—if only we choose to inhale.

So when the moments come when we feel like dirt or unin-spired clay, or when a cloud of darkness causes us to forget that our breathing matters, let's eavesdrop on each other. There are brilliant, beautiful people all around us, who have light and dark wisdom hov-ering over the depths of their souls as an offering to our own. Rather than fretting about what we are not, we can choose to breathe in and be inspired. And maybe put on some red lipstick, just because.

Q & R

1. Practice increasing your awareness of the spirit of the people around you, including yourself. Notice the ones who breathe life into you; notice whom you seem to inspire. Spend time each day reflecting on this and record your observations in your journal. This small activity can cultivate the brightness of the light you bring to the world around you.

2. What parts of you are dry and longing to be inspired by infinite potential? Ask God right now to breathe into you his new life.

3. What would your life look like if you were inspired by others rather than fretting about what you are not?

* * *

CHAPTER 10

Magic in Brooklyn:
Cultivating Timeless Delight

In eighth grade, Drea decided that we were going to be friends. I had just moved to town. So it sounded like a good idea to me.

It was one of the best decisions I never made.

We couldn't be more different. Drea is bold and unafraid to ask for what she wants. Not to mention that she is fiercely smart and unapologetically herself. The thing I love most about her is that she reshapes the world to work for her. Nothing scares her.

Growing up, she was the rebellious one who tried everything, dated a lot of boys, and lived all over the world learning languages and making lifelong friends. Wherever she is, things come to life. She brings people together. Opportunities come to light. Friends become family.

You can see why I love her.

Drea has been a constant source of light and love in my life, and in many ways we have been one another's safe place when storms come in. When I was in tenth grade and withering away to nothing because my body was the only thing I had control over, she and her mom lit candles at St. Peter's and made chocolate molé for me. When she confessed to her parents that she got a speeding ticket while ditching school and driving an hour away to go shopping with her boyfriend, she ran away to my house until the storm blew over.

Through the years, there have been lots of times when life felt uncertain or we hurt each other's feelings. But instead of running from friendship, we chose to show up for one another and trust that our friendship has the power to make both of us better.

I know it is true for me. When my kids were little, I remember lying in bed next to Joe and having this moment of panic because I couldn't think of anything I enjoyed doing. I remember feeling like each day was running together, and I was so consumed by the monotony that I had lost myself. I couldn't tell you what I enjoyed, what I loved, what I delighted in. I love my kids so much I wanted to eat them up, but I felt like I was waking up from a few years of being so sleep deprived and busy with everyone's needs that I had forgotten what I delighted in and who I was without these beloved creatures.

My little crisis had started earlier in the day when I realized I had just yelled at the kids for laughing too loudly. At the time, all three of my children were sharing a room. I was in the kitchen, try- ing to get dinner started, and my kids were in their room playing nicely but really loudly. There were shrieks of delight, the pound- ing of little feet, and so much laughter. Usually I would enjoy these sounds and my kids' joy-filled camaraderie (they were getting along!), but for whatever reason I wanted quiet. So I yelled at them to stop laughing. And as the words were coming out of my mouth, I realized something was wrong with my soul. I was so worn down that I had lost my ability to appreciate laughter. At that moment, I realized I needed to regain a sense of celebration. To reawaken delight in my own life.

One event that helped me regain my sense of delight hap- pened a few months after yelling at my kids to stop laughing, and it involved Drea.

Drea met Hal on OkCupid. Hal is a lifelong New Yorker, a renowned photographer, and one of the best cooks you'll ever meet. Not to mention he has played leap frog with Iggy Pop. That sums up the awesomeness that is Hal. Drea and Hal took a bike ride together, and she thought he was interesting. They touched knees at a movie, and she realized that not only was he interesting but he was also super hot. Fast forward a few months, and they both decided that forever sounded like a good idea.

A wedding was planned for October.

This is where it all started, both their marriage and my return to life.

On the second Thursday in October, my mom (who loves Drea like a daughter) and I took off to Brooklyn for a girls' weekend and a wedding. While we were there, we slept in a big fluffy bed and stayed up late drinking champagne. We ate cheap pizza and cannolis. I made a toast to new friends and danced so much at the reception that my neck was sore from where my chunky brides-maid necklace had bounced against my chest all night. It was a weekend of feasting for my soul.

I have a lot of favorite memories from that weekend. Traveling with my mom is always a good time. Getting ready at Parker's house reminded me of how women are really good at caring for one another. Sharing a meal with Nadia and Jomar and Zefrey, Drea's closest New York friends, made me realize how truly great she is at friendship. But by far the most meaningful moment for me happened because of the rain.

Plans to have the wedding ceremony outside had to be changed at the last minute, thanks to a cool drizzly storm. All the festivities were moved inside, which meant that the poles of the Chuppah (yes, Drea married a good Jewish boy), designed to be staked into the ground, would now have to be set up inside on a slippery wooden stage. The Chuppah, an important part of a Jewish wed-ding ceremony, is a four-cornered canopy made from cloth that symbolizes the roof of the home the couple will make together, the fabric of their bedcovers, and the protection of God's love. Inside on the stage, the poles of the Chuppah mimicked the legs of a newborn giraffe. They worked but needed to be steadied. A solution had to be found because the Chuppah was so not optional.

We made a plan for the ceremony. After walking down the aisle to take our places on the stage, I steadied one side of the Chuppah, while a groomsman steadied the other side. Drea and Hal stood under it, all gorgeous and glowy. Instead of standing in a long line of bridesmaids, I ended up next to Drea, almost touching shoulders with her as I held up her Chuppah.

Because that is what we do for one another. We hold up love and home and goodness when life gets unsteady.

It was a magical moment.

Have you ever had a moment when time slows down, and you can see with clarity the magic happening all around you? I remember as a kid playing outside and not even realizing it was getting dark. I was so present in the game that it didn't even occur to me that the light was changing. There have been similar moments in my adult life, like when Joe and I have been making out and didn't realize how much time had passed. Being in the moment created a sense of timelessness.

Some of my favorite theologians postulate that this sense of timelessness is a prophetic groaning of heaven. I like that idea, that we can stretch time out a bit. Slow it down. Fit more of life into its cracks and crevices.

When we deliberately make space in our lives for timeless delight, we get to enjoy something so deeply that we never want the moment to end. What is happening inside and what is happening all around us are completely synced for a brief moment, so much so that it feels sacred.

In Celtic spirituality, they have a term for this phenomenon: *liminal space*. The line between earth and heaven is so thin, it is hard to tell where one ends and the other begins. I think another word for this experience is *feasting*. And it happens for me when I cultivate opportunities to be extravagant, to give generously, and to become so consumed by delight that I don't realize it is getting dark outside.

Experiencing this sense of liminal space takes some intentionality. When we are young, we know what we love and what we love to do. We don't measure our value by what we have or what our titles are. Instead, we are simply us.

As we grow and become full-fledged adults, our hearts change a little. Wouldn't it be interesting if the question that told us the most about one another was, "What do you love?" instead of "What do you do?" That is the gift Drea gives to me every time I see her. She reminds me of how to delight, how to enjoy. Being around her reminds me who I am.

Over those four magical days celebrating Drea and Hal, I remembered that feasting is an opportunity to regain our equilibrium. Showing up to celebrate and dancing our buns off and experiencing a reprieve from our daily routines—it breathes life into our souls. The beat of the music that draws us to the dance floor is like the pulse of life itself. It seems to me that God's Spirit winks at us and beckons us to get up and dance to the music that's been playing in our souls all along.

But this movement requires us to change our posture. For me, it meant flying to Brooklyn. It will mean something different for you. Wherever your feasting takes you, notice when the beat of your heart syncs with the rhythm of divine goodness. May camaraderie and delight illuminate your worn-down places. May you laugh with abandon. And may you commit to friends who will be eternally grateful they were chosen to be yours.

P.S. Drea and Hal came to visit us in Denver the summer after they got married. She came to tell me the news they were having a baby. I pulled out a gift I had already bought a few weeks before; something inside me knew already. Because life ties us together in ways we don't fully understand. Timelessness.

Q & R

1. How has the beautiful cacophony of motherhood caused you to lose sight of what you delight in for your own life?

2. Reflect on "timeless" moments you have experienced.

3. How does your posture need to change in order to invite more?

4. What do you love? What brings you alive (dancing, celebrating, connecting, traveling)?

5. What would your friends from different eras of your life say you delighted in?

* * *

CHAPTER 11

Sabbath like a Sunrise:
Restoring Our Weary Places

It's a quiet, rainy Thursday morning, and I'm still in my pajamas. I am ignoring the dishes in the sink and allowing myself to linger a little. This is not my normal hectic morning routine of rushing kids to the bus stop and heading straight into work. This change of rhythm is life-giving.

Sometimes I don't realize what a hectic pace I keep until I lounge in my jammies for a morning, while the house is so quiet I can actually hear my own heart beating.

The world beats to a predictable rhythm. The moon rises and sets, as does the sun, seasons shift four times a year, and our bodies ebb and flow to a lunar cycle. We live by an inhale, exhale, inhale, exhale rhythm—but we rarely stop to notice it. It is in those rare moments when we pause to listen that our heartbeat syncs to the heartbeat of creation, and we remember there is a pattern of living and resting that offers respite to our weary bones.

Finding a healthy rhythm in our lives is essential for resetting our equilibrium. When we don't rest, it is often because we have come to believe that the entire world rests on our shoulders. Our to-do list controls our pace. But sometimes we need a break from the churning of life's priorities to find the rhythm that uniquely suits our soul.

I get to talk with a lot of women over the course of a year, and almost always they will share with me about their lives. (That is something I love about women; we are really good at confiding in one another.) Without fail, almost every woman tells me one of two things. The first is that they are exhausted, and the second is that they feel like they aren't doing enough with their lives.

Exhausted because they are doing so much and terrified that they aren't doing enough.

And it isn't true only for the women I meet, but for the friends I know best. My friend Maggie stays at home with her four kids and sleeps only a handful of hours a night so she can run an Etsy shop from her house. Lacey is running a CrossFit gym with her husband and just had a new baby. Mikkee works a full-time job in four days a week and then, because she doesn't have any kids of her own, has chosen to move in with her best friend Stephanie in order to help Stephanie and her husband raise their kids. In her "spare time," she takes on as many freelance writing projects as possible. Tara volunteers at her kid's preschool so often that one of the other parents thought she was a paid teacher.

One would assume that each of my friends would be filled with a sense of accomplishment, but instead their insides swirl with doubt. They often worry that they are failing at life.

It hurts my guts to talk with so many women who feel like they aren't thriving. But just a few days ago, I was talking to a friend who not so diplomatically reminded me that I am feeling the same things. Like how I can't sleep through the night, because I wake up worrying about all the things in my life that need worrying about. Or how I have needed to start saying no to commitments for a really long time, but haven't because I don't want to let people down.

It feels to me like we, as a generation of sisters who are raising the world together, might need to call a time-out. To bring everyone in for a huddle and find more life-giving ways to move through the world. Because there are too many of us who are waking up at three o'clock in the morning and abusing ourselves for everything we aren't—aren't doing, aren't being. We are so busy that we are losing the ability to be human—to live at a sane pace, to have long conversations with pregnant pauses where no one feels rushed to fill the silence, to linger enough to appreciate the smell of orange blossoms blooming in the spring.

It seems to me that we need less striving and more life.

So if this is you: If you crave deeper friendships, but don't feel like you have the time or energy for them; if you feel like you haven't taken a deep breath in years; if you are exhausted and craving rest; if you feel depleted by giving so much to the world around you that you have forgotten how to care for yourself . . . then I have an idea for you. For us. I believe that our collective solution is found in a word called *Sabbath*, coupled with becoming religious about play.

Sabbath is a concept that comes from our Jewish friends. They recognize that God has instructed us to rest, and they take that very seriously. So every week they spend a full twenty-four hours slowing down and deliberately focusing on rest. Not only that, but if you were to go to Israel for the Sabbath you would find that at the end of the twenty-four hours of rest they celebrate like it is Christmas and Easter all wrapped into one. In other words, they rest and play. And they do this every single week.

Our monastic fathers believed there are two ways to meet God. The first is through radical love; the second is through radical self-sacrifice. I believe the same thing is true when it comes to Sabbath. It seems to me there are two ways to experience the restoration of our weary places and to observe a regular rhythm of rest. The first one is to be still and the second is to play.

Being still is probably the one most of us are familiar with in some way. It is the practice of deliberately choosing moments of solitude, fasting, or slowing down in order to recalibrate the rhythm of our soul. I like to think of it as choosing darkness for a day or a season. Choosing less stimulation, less entertainment, less time around other people, less glaring light. It is making space for the quiet that comes with darkness in order to be better prepared to choose what light we let back in when our stillness is over.

Since childhood, many of us have resented the idea of rest. Maybe we were afraid of missing out on something fun, or resting meant confronting our fear of the dark. Even as an adult, I hate to risk missing out on fun. This fear trickles down into all areas of my life so much so that saying no to any invitation feels like a knife wound. Carving out time to be still becomes an exercise in being comfortable with not being the center of attention, with knowing that stillness is healing the parts of my soul that think they need the distraction of fun but might benefit from the quiet of stillness instead.

My fears of the dark also surface when I have to confront why I have chosen the crazy pace I am keeping. Too often, I am choosing a full-out sprint because I am afraid of what I might feel if I slow down. Changing my pace forces me to sit face-to-face with my unhealthy need for achievement and affirmation. When I look these monsters in the eye, they seem much less scary than they did when I was trying to outrun them.

Being still is a reminder of how life and light emerge out of the darkness of primal silence. Our souls always benefit from periods of intentional stillness.

And then there is play.

I am an introvert who comes from a faith tradition that admires people who can sit still and be quiet for a long time. I love spending time by myself in quiet and could convince myself that this is my rest language—but the truth is, it usually isn't good for me. I am better around people who can remind me who I am.

I was talking with a good friend of mine named Jared about this, and he shared with me about a conversation he had with a spiritual director. He was telling his spiritual director about how he had decided to incorporate more silence and solitude into his life. But his mentor looked at him while he was talking and said, "Well, why would you do that?" Jared's reply was, "Because it's really good for me and I need to figure some things out." The response of his director surprised him. "Why don't you do the things that are really life-giving to you? Like, go have a meal with good people and paint pictures and just enjoy life. Play." Jared shared that it was an interesting reorienting of what he needed at that point in his life.

I think sometimes we need to hear, "Be still and quiet." And I think sometimes we need to hear, "Go play and be with people." When we understand that rest isn't just silence and solitude but rather anything that gives us life, it makes the concept of slowing down so much less threatening. I love this quote by Eugene Peterson in *Run with the Horses*:

> There it is—"new every morning; great is your faithfulness." God's persistence is not a dogged repetition of duty. It has all the surprise and all the creativity and yet all the certainty and regularity of a new day. Sunrise—when the spontaneous and the certain arrive at the same time.[1]

That last line is what I think a rhythm of rest *can* look like. It should be certain and also spontaneous. Like the sunrise. We can set our clock to its rhythms, yet it can surprise us with different shades of color. So I think it's important to find rhythms that are scheduled but not forced, things that are life-giving and not a burden. And that is going to look different for each of us.

---

1   Eugene H. Peterson, *Run with the Horses: The Quest for Life at Its Best* (Downers Grove: InterVarsity Press, 2010), 116.

Let me offer a few thoughts that might spark ideas on how to rest and play.

Start doing things you love to do. An acquaintance recently asked me what my hobbies are. I had no answers. So I started thinking about what kind of hobbies I would *like* to have. Then I thought back to the things I was drawn to as a kid, because I believe that some of our birthright gifts are evident even as kids. When I was a child, I loved to dance, so I have decided to start taking dance lessons as a Sabbath practice. Now I know this sounds ridiculous to some of you who have really littles at home and are so exhausted that you can barely make yourself a cup of coffee in the morning. To you I say: your hobby is sleep. There will be time for other life-giving activities later.

Make a list. Every month, my family makes a list of "play day" activities to do together. We usually come up with a handful of ideas, and then on the days we have set aside for play we refer to our list. This helps eliminate the "what should we do?" dilemma. This particular month, we want to go horseback riding, eat cannolis, build a snow igloo, and take our dogs for a long hike.

Redefine your understanding of rest. This one might hurt a little. Maybe we need to recalibrate our understanding of rest. You guys, we are on our devices. All. The. Freaking. Time. The problem is that rest isn't binge watching TV; it isn't checking out for hours on end. Distractions are different than rest. I can spend an hour looking at BuzzFeed on my phone, but that doesn't give me life. It distracts me from life. Rest is participating in things that are rejuvenating. Make a list of the distractions you choose and analyze whether they are contributing to your own soul care or just delaying it.

Sync with the rhythms of nature. Sometimes we need a break in a beautiful place to figure everything out. The voice of nature is what I prefer. When is the last time you walked around barefoot? Or grabbed a blanket and laid out under the stars? Maybe nature is where you will get in touch with the rhythms of the universe. Get outside and walk in the mud. Forget about the laundry. Seriously. It is never going to be finished. That is the truth. Let it pile up for a day. It will be waiting for you after you have rested.

One last thing. Don't be surprised that, if you start to choose rest and play, you experience all the feelings. All. Of. The. Feelings. You might need to address the fact that rest feels indulgent, or the feelings of anxiety or shame that arise when you don't feel productive. Emotions that have been drowned out by the background noise of busyness come to the surface when we slow down. My own demons of not being able to say no because I am such a people pleaser raise their ugly heads when I practice rest. They tell me I am losing; I am missing something. But what I am missing is just the adrenaline rush of busy. And busy isn't a pace I can keep forever.

It takes courage to rest and play, because Sabbath keeping requires relaxing into humble, human rhythms. To practice Sabbath means to go quiet, to be less noticed, to stop striving, and to rest in the ordinary. As difficult as this may be, our souls need it like our bodies need oxygen.

So to all my sisters who feel weary, to those of us who are worried we are screwing things up, or who feel like we are too exhausted to face the day, or who lay awake at night creating lists . . .

May we throw off the burden of doing too much, so we can enjoy the freedom of stillness and play.

May we deliberately change the rhythms of our lives, as we listen to the sound of our own hearts beating.

May we celebrate the certain spontaneity of a sunrise.

Q & R

1. How would you describe the pace of your life?

2. How hard would it be to press "pause" on your to-do list? What do you feel when you think about slowing down?

3. When during the week can you practice intentional stillness?

4. What were your childhood hobbies?

5. What are your present-day hobbies?

6. Make a list of rejuvenating play-day activities for your family (or just yourself, or you and your spouse).

7. List five ways you can connect with nature this month.

8. Evaluate your relationship with your technological devices. How connected to them are you? How have they mimicked rest for you? Can you create a rhythm around when you use your devices?

⋆ ⋆ ⋆

CHAPTER 12

The Womb Time That Winter Brings:
Surrendering to
Nature's Rhythms

I can remember the day we met, each moment etched into my memory because you were the first. The first one to hold the space, the first one to bear witness to my heartbeat as yours was learning its rhythm just a few inches below my own.

I was only twenty-two when I found out that you had taken residency. It was the deepest of winter, the middle of December, as I sat on the floor of the shower and sobbed because I was still a baby myself—and how in the world could I have been so careless. The truth I didn't know on the floor of the shower that day is that you were the one who was bringing me to life. And while I feared everything would change, I wasn't prepared for the miracle that happened over the next nine months, as soul and body were woven together in the darkness that womb-time offers. Your gestation of body mimicked my gestation toward motherhood. And as we worked together in a hospital room in Southern California, to stretch and push through the darkness into the light of your dad's arms and the witnessing eyes of Nene and Uncle Charley and Grandma Joan and all the people who love us best, I couldn't help but realize that it is in the deepest winter that the gift of new life is born.

These are the words I wrote to my firstborn a few months after he came home from the hospital. He entered into the world of light and breath during late September, so by the time December came around again we were well acquainted with one another. It was right around the time of the winter solstice, the longest night of the year in the northern hemisphere, when we, just the two of us, a newly formed team, had taken up our nighttime ritual of waking at 2:00 a.m. to nourish his growing body, while I studied his face by moonlight. It was a peaceful, magic-filled season, in which we did as much living by moonlight as we did by sunlight.

Since those long nights in December many years ago, every winter solstice reminds me how beautiful the long nights of winter can be. The reason the northern hemisphere experiences this longest night is that the sun has moved south below the equator as far as it can go, and now it will stand still (*solstice* means "sun stand still") for three days before it starts on its journey back up north. This feels like a prophetic glimpse into a redeeming Son who spent three days lying still in a tomb before rising again.

Nature is a storyteller infused with holy narratives. Maybe this is why so many faith traditions find the darkest time of year to be deeply spiritual. The winter solstice in particular is a day when seeking people throughout the world follow rituals to take notice of this long, dark night. *The Essene Book of Days* explains, "Ancient people used this time of 'longest night' to focus on the power of darkness. Not the negative image of darkness, but the richness of that unknown, dark, fertile, deep part in each of us wherein our intuitive, creative forces abide."[1]

Just as life is woven together in the darkness of a womb, so too can our lives find gestation in the long dark of winter.

---

1   Danaan Parry, *The Essene Book of Days 2003* (Washington: Earthstewards Network Publications, 2002), 391.

I'll be honest—I have to work hard to maintain my equilibrium during winter. Winter makes me sad; it is usually the time when I start to feel like I need to visit my counselor again. Or my intense struggle with anxiety surfaces. Or I feel like I need to quit my job because it is all just too much.

Winter feels uncomfortable for me because I am always fighting against it. On days when it is below zero, I will walk outside, take in a deep breath, and feel every muscle of my body tense up in an attempt to shield my skin from the harshness of the air. I instinctively clench my jaw and my shoulders as my natural response to the discomfort that surrounds me. But I can't live life clenched, constantly worried about being uncomfortable. So I am learning to make peace with cold, dark days. To relax my shivering muscles and to allow my chest to take big full breaths . . . and then to breathe out all my tension. The cold may not be comfortable, but sometimes life is about finding consolation in places of discomfort.

I can't help but wonder: If our bodies reflect the lunar rhythm in a world that pulses with a predictable cycle through four distinct seasons, then why don't we adapt our daily pace to reflect what nature is living all around us? So often, the pace we keep presses against nature's tempos. Productivity and maximizing each moment of every day has blindfolded our instincts. I believe that the natural world holds truths that, in our haste to become civilized, have been forgotten. Herbs and petals grow as medicine all around us, but we rush to the pharmacy to treat our symptoms. As women we often forget that our bodies reflect a lunar cycle of waxing and waning.

It seems to me that if we are to begin to notice and honor the natural rhythms of the universe, it will take a guttural sense of humility: an acknowledgement that the earth has existed for lifetimes before we breathed our first breath and will continue to exist long after we are gone. The ground underneath us right now has seen wonders of nature and civilization that our eyes will never see.

I love that the word *humble* is derived from the Latin word *humus*, which means "ground or dirt." Humility, then—a coming to grips with our humanity and recognizing that we live in nature and are made of it—is the first step in owning that we may have things to learn from the womb of the earth that sustains us.

What would it look like if we started to welcome the ebb and flow of our internal and external seasons, so that we could come back into relationship with the rhythms of nature?

I began asking myself that question when my family and I moved from San Diego to Denver. By our second full winter in our new state, I realized that winter demands a different pace of living. So why was this so hard for me?

My intense need to achieve was the culprit. I felt the need to maintain a constant pace, and when the cold or darkness threatened to slow me down, I pushed harder to maintain, pretending that nothing should impede my ability to be productive. Especially in the month of December, when I was going crazy doing, buying, and showing up for the commitments and events the holidays necessitate. While I was running around at a breakneck pace, the ground was still and quiet; the magic of gestation was happening just below the surface. The days were short and the nights were long, but I continued at a pace worthy of high summer and wondered why I was tired and depressed. This is how I realized I was not utilizing the seasons effectively. In particular, I was missing out on the regenerative process that winter offers.

Last winter I found myself lying in bed, unable to push the covers back, so worn out that my body shouted to me and demanded that I rest. I conceded. I slept for a whole day and then laid in bed for a whole day after that. I stared at the barren trees and monochrome landscape outside my window. I read books that had been sitting on my shelf, waiting for the spare moment that I always anticipated happening but never did. And that short period of two days, resting and daydreaming—luxuries I rarely allowed—restored my energy. The landscape outside reminded me that my own internal rhythm needed winter just as much as the world around me did. My soul and body longed to be in sync with the intentional time of rest and darkness. I needed to surrender to the womb time winter brings and to learn to appreciate the gift of darkness, as it invited me inward to restore my weary places.

Just as the earth experiences the long dark nights of midwinter, so too can our spiritual life. When I began to harmonize my life with the cycles of the seasons rather than pretending the different energies shouldn't affect me, I noticed my inner life recalibrate in profound ways. One realization was that my spiritual life reflected the seasonal tides more than I was initially comfortable with. This meant I had to realize that, just like the different seasons offer more or less light, so too the divine light available to me ebbs and flows. There have been seasons in my journey with God that have felt like winter. And when the light was bleak, I furiously rubbed sticks together, trying to manufacture warmth and light. But my efforts were futile, because no matter how hard I tried to coerce the divine light, it was committed to a time of solstice. I learned that the long dark night wasn't something to fight against. Rather, my job was to sit and rest without fear of the sun not returning in due time. I realized that I can trust the divine ebb and flow of light that is God's presence.

I like these ideas, mostly because I am always looking for opportunities to infuse the ordinary with the holy. Here are some of the ways I have practiced surrendering to solstice energy.

Contemplating darkness. Darkness is soothing when I am exhausted and want to take a nap. I can think of numerous times when I was stuck in an airport due to delayed flights and felt desperate for a nap. Simply putting a sweatshirt over my eyes to block out the light was a small miracle. During the time of winter solstice,

I intentionally recall the times when darkness was a gift. I create a ritual on the evening of the solstice, turning off all lights as the sun starts to set. I light a few candles and spend the evening reflecting on dark and light.

Burning and setting ablaze. I begin the evening of the solstice in darkness. I feel the darkness, the cold, the aloneness. Then I light a fire and feel the warmth and light that it brings. I get two pieces of paper, and on the first, I write down things I need to rid myself of—fears, anxieties, addictions, distractions. Then I burn that page in the fire. On the second page, I invite new light and inspiration into my heart as I enter mindfully into a new season. I pray over that page, asking God to set it ablaze, and for the fire to burn with warmth, strength, and passion. I end this ritual by giving thanks and gathering with people with whom I love to tell stories and share good conversation about our hopes for the future.

Taking a night walk. I notice the inky black sky and how early darkness has come. I appreciate how the stars and moon are offering their beauty during the prolonged evening.

Listening to my body. I allow it to rest, to sleep, to warm itself. Often it feels indulgent or selfish to care for myself. How can I find the time to take care of my body and soul when all the other bodies around me have such pressing needs? It seems to me that somewhere along the journey we women have decided it is okay to run ourselves ragged as long as everyone else is taken care of. Maybe it is time to call a truce. To listen to what our bodies are saying. And just as we rush to care for a crying baby or a hungry toddler, we extend that same care to ourselves. We come home to ourselves and remember that our bodies and souls need the same care we give to the people we love the most.

Reading inspiring literature. I choose readings that birth creative imagery into the gray scale of the winter landscape. One of my favorites is this poem by Joyce Rupp:

"WINTER'S CLOAK"

This year I do not want
the dark to leave me.
I need its wrap
of silent stillness,
its cloak
of long lasting embrace.
Too much light
has pulled me away
from the chamber
of gestation.
Let the dawns
come late,
let the sunsets
arrive early,
let the evenings
extend themselves
while I lean into
the abyss of my being.
Let me lie in the cave
of my soul,
for too much light
blinds me,
steals the source
of revelation.
Let me seek solace
in the empty places
of winter's passage,
those vast dark nights
that never fail to shelter me.[2]

---

2   Joyce Rupp and Macrina Wiederkehr, *Circle of Life: The Heart's Journey through the Seasons* (Notre Dame, IN: Sorin Books, 2005), 249. Reprinted by permission of the publisher.

The rhythms of the earth are offering to guide each of us. May we let them do their work. The womb time that winter brings lends life to our bodies and breath to our souls.

Q & R

1. Have you resisted or lamented the longest, darkest nights of the year?

2. How can you alter your expectations and pace to better sync with the rhythms of your body and the seasons?

3. When you are in deep need of rest this winter, can you humbly and bravely call in reinforcements for yourself? Can you write down a concrete, detailed plan to do so?

4. What activities and rest times feel appropriate for you in each season?

5. At the change of each season, are you willing to pause and audit what is not working in your life, and what beauty and goodness needs to be added in?

6. Have you experienced the ebb and flow of God's presence in your life? How would you benefit by treating these times with acceptance and faith?

* * *

CHAPTER 13

A Constellation of Reasons:

Extracting Truth from the Natural World

Do you have magical places in your life? A space you return to when you need to be lifted up or healed? Over the years, my places have looked different: a dirt path, a cove in Maui, a constellation in the shape of a man with a water jug.

At certain points in our lives, we have a deep longing for answers. I am convinced that what we are looking for in these moments can be found in the cathedral of earth, sea, and sky. That there are truths we can find only by digging in dirt, wading in water, breathing in air, and looking at the stars.

One of my favorite books is *The Rebirthing of God* by John Philip Newell. He begins with a conversation about pilgrimage and the idea of "coming back into relationship with Earth as sacred."[1] He explains that the ancient Celts spoke of the great living cathedral of earth, sea, and sky. They believed that nature has secrets to share, and that the outside world is just as good a place to encounter God as any church building.

---

1   John Phillip Newell, *The Rebirthing of God: Christianity's Struggle for New Beginnings* (Woodstock, VT: Skylight Paths Publishing, 2014), xiv.

When we wonder what it means to flourish, maybe it is the totality of the universe that gives us a lesson in thriving. And when we wonder why we are here on this huge spinning globe, and whether our lives mean something, maybe going outside is the simplest way to find our answers.

Earth. Appreciating the cathedral of Earth is about noticing the places where we put our feet and how we rely on the dirt to sustain us. For a few years, we lived down the road from a steep and rocky hill, accessed by a hidden path. The initial trek up the hill is so steep that I always felt like I was going to throw up from exhaustion before I made it to the summit. Thankfully, the path eventually flattens out and begins to wind over the top ridge of the mountain. Most mornings, my dog Oliver and I would start our day with a hike. Long before any of my littles were rubbing sleep from their eyes and asking for breakfast, we were communing with the dusty trail.

At that time of morning, we would often stumble upon a pack of coyotes nestled in among the thistle and rocks, winding down from their nighttime hunting rituals. With the daylight gathering over the hill, they were sleepy and only a little interested in us. After a lot of days of sizing one another up, we all mostly trusted that we could coexist without much fuss. So we just hiked right by them. One morning, we encountered a large rattlesnake right in the middle of the path. It was sunning itself, trying to soak up the first heat of the morning. Ollie startled it with a bunch of sniffing and barking, the snake hissed and coiled, and Ollie realized it was best to leave it alone. We kept hiking.

These morning hikes came at a time in my life when things felt like they were falling apart. We were in the middle of losing a business we owned. Our finances were a mess, and things between Joe and I were strained. One morning, I was hiking and praying desperate prayers when I felt compelled to kneel. I don't know what came over me, and I was worried that someone else would be hiking and find me lying in the dirt. How would I explain this to a fellow hiker?

I decided it wouldn't be the first time I did something weird. So I kneeled with my forehead to the ground. In the dirt. In utter surrender.

For months afterward, all through the spring and summer, Oliver and I would start our mornings by hiking to the top of the hill, where I would kneel in the dirt, and he would sniff every rock he could. Pressing my forehead to the ground, I would pray for perspective, for glimmers of hope in the darkness. Some days I didn't have any words; on others, I pleaded with God for enough light for the day. My prayer altar was a dirt path; my fellow worshipers were coyotes, rattle snakes, and a dog. When my time in the dirt was done, I would pick myself up, wipe the dust from my forehead, and head back down the hill with the sun rising straight in front of me. The light was so bright that I would close my eyes and just let the warmth hit my face for a few moments.

Humans are meant to touch the earth. With our bare skin. From walking barefoot outside to digging in the garden, sitting in the wilderness, or sleeping out under the stars, contact with the earth has become a much smaller part of daily life for us than it was for previous generations. Many healing traditions, like Chinese medicine and Ayurveda, have understood the importance of skin contact with dirt for well-being. Now science is starting to catch up with these ancient healing practices that connect human beings to the earth beneath their feet. The benefits of grounding are numerous, from improving sleep and reducing stress to normalizing circadian rhythms and reducing inflammation. Being outside and touching the dirt not only heals our bodies, but reminds us that God has created us to be close to the earth.

Sea. I knew that I didn't have a choice. I had to jump. Joe had already made the leap, and now it was my turn. Lori, my

STARRY-EYED

sister-in-law, was waiting behind me, high up at the top of Black Rock. We had arrived in Maui a few days earlier, and ever since touching down on the tarmac I knew this moment was coming. The rocks were sharp on my feet, and wading in the water below were a dozen local Hawaiians who—it was obvious—were very comfortable with the leap. They were challenging each other to do backflips while I was contemplating if I could jump at all. I knew that waiting too long would wreck my confidence, and, seeing my kids on the beach with hopeful eyes, I pushed off the side with one foot and pencil dove into the water below.

What is it about jumping off tall rocks into water that makes you feel like you are really living?

After I jumped, Lori made the leap, and we high-fived like we had just landed on the moon. Joseph, my thirteen-year-old, decided to give it a try next, which inspired Josh, my eleven-year-old nephew, to jump as well.

Joseph climbed up and jumped. That is the kind of person he is. He takes after his dad.

Then it was Josh's turn.

Interspersed with all our cliff jumping shenanigans were the native Hawaiian teenagers, treading water and jumping alongside us. They were talking smack to one another—peppered with plenty of F-bombs and crude jokes.

Josh climbed to the top of the rock and stood still. And kept on standing, his feet frozen to the rock. Lori looked at me with eyes that bled for her son. She knew that backing down from this challenge would haunt him. And so she mobilized our smack-talking, crude-joke-cracking, water-treading teenage companions into action. She swam over to the splash zone and explained that her son Josh was struggling to make the jump. Then she asked them to join her in cheering him on.

Those dudes became some of my favorite people on the planet

96

as they whooped and hollered, calling out, "Josh, you've got this!" Tears filled my eyes at this fresh evidence of how awesome people can be. Josh was baffled that all these guys knew his name. He became the most powerful eleven-year-old in the world at that moment.

He jumped.

As he surfaced, his new buddies high-fived him and told him how brave he was. He smiled about that experience for the rest of the week. And I'm pretty sure, deep down, that moment made him a little braver and a little more whole. I know it did for me.

Water has the ability to usher in new life. When a pregnant woman's water breaks, it is a sign that new life is being birthed into the world. When we choose to be baptized, it is a symbol of being cleansed and of choosing new life. The earth that surrounds us is made fertile by falling rain. Water brings life. Cleansing. Renewal.

If there is a part of your life that longs for refreshment or renewal, the cathedral of Sea has life-giving properties to offer. In order to float in its wisdom, how about jumping off a tall cliff into a lake or ocean, or skinny-dipping under the light of the moon? A less thrilling but just as meaningful practice may be sipping a cup of warm tea and appreciating the warmth and refreshment water gives.

Sky. Did you know that the universe has such a predictable rhythm that we can calculate the position of the stars and planets back tens of thousands of years? We know what constellations King Tut saw out his window during the first summer he reigned. By studying the history of the cosmos, we have learned about the pattern of the seasons and have created our own measurement of time along with our calendar system, all based on the magnificent movement of the universe.

Isn't it interesting that throughout recorded history, humans have looked to the sky for answers? Not only about our current situation, but also for insight into our future and past. I believe this is an acknowledgment that something deep and vast is contained in the cosmos. Not only as women do our bodies reflect the cycle of the moon, but scientists are convinced that we are all made of stars.

PBS aired a series in the eighties called *Cosmos*, in which astronomer Carl Sagan hosted and narrated thirteen episodes about the origins of the cosmos. One of the most famous quotes that came out of the series is this reflection by Sagan: "We are a way for the universe to know itself. Some part of our being knows this is where we came from. We long to return. And we can—because the cosmos is also within us. We're made of star stuff."

Literally.

Here is the science behind this theory.

All organic matter, including our bodies, is made of carbon, nitrogen, and oxygen atoms. Stars are made of hydrogen, helium, and carbon. When a star burns out, it dies in a violent explosion called a nova, or if it is a big star, a supernova. This explosion throws a large cloud of dust and gas into space. This cloud contracts under its own gravity and begins to collect into molecules like water, and eventually into every element in the periodic table aside from hydrogen. (Hydrogen was the first and simplest atom to exist; it precedes every other element.) These molecules, born of stars, are the very ones that make up all organic life on earth.

"It's a well-tested theory," says Chris Impey, a professor of astronomy at the University of Arizona. "We know that stars make heavy elements, and late in their lives, they eject gas into the medium between stars so it can be part of subsequent stars and planets (and people). So, all life on Earth and the atoms in our bodies were created in the furnace of now-long-dead stars."[2]

---

2   Remy Melina, "Are We Really All Made of Stars?," *LiveScience*, 13 October 2010, http://www.livescience.com/32828-humans-really-made-stars.html.

We are connected to the cosmos. It is no wonder we look to it for insights into our past, present, and future. Throughout history, humans have even depended on the stars for help making daily choices. Sailors have looked to the stars to navigate oceans, farmers consult the sky when deciding when to plant crops, and spiritual seekers were introduced to a new King, thanks to a single star shining brightly in the sky. Looking to the sky helps to sync us to the world's mysteries—things like navigating unknown frontiers and harnessing time.

Modern existence is filled with many conveniences that disconnect us from the sky. We have artificial light to illuminate the night; the moon is just a nice accessory. We have GPS, so no need to consult the stars for navigational help. We consult the calendar on our phone to find out when summer officially starts. In the midst of these conveniences, I wonder if we have lost our sense of wonder at the miraculous things that happen all around this spinning ball of dirt we live on.

We are floating in a universe that dazzles with the touch of an artist, but we are sometimes too distracted to appreciate it. Paul Hawken writes, "Ralph Waldo Emerson once asked what we would do if the stars only came out once every thousand years. No one would sleep that night, of course. The world would create new religions overnight. We would be ecstatic, delirious, and made rapturous by the glory of God. Instead, the stars come out every night and we watch television."[3]

How do we find wonder in the sky? I think it might have something to do with dots and lines. It makes sense to me that the way we represent constellations on paper is with dot-and-line drawings. Just like those connect-the-dots drawings we remember from

---

3   Paul Hawken, "Commencement: Healing or Stealing?," commencement address at the University of Portland, 03 May 2009, www.up.edu/commencement/default.aspx?cid=9456.

childhood, the full picture is unrecognizable until all the dots have been connected. The same thing is true of our lives.

Have you ever taken a moment to write down all the most important or memorable moments that have shaped you? I like to think of these moments as stars in the still-forming constellation of my life. These experiences shine through the monotony of everyday life. Mapping your own constellation may take a few days or even a few months. Once you have spent a good amount of time extracting every important star-moment from your memory, the next step is to connect the dots. This is when you will discover what shape your dots connect to reveal what your constellation looks like. Draw some lines, look for themes that keep coming up or patterns that emerge. The cathedral of Sky has insights to share with you.

Nature is infused with the holy. It has fingerprints of the divine pressed into the dirt, swirling in the ocean, and glimmering in the sky.

So . . .

Let's hear it from Sky,
With Earth joining in,
And a huge round of applause from Sea.
Let Wilderness turn cartwheels,
Animals, come dance,
Put every tree of the forest in the choir—
An extravaganza before GOD as he comes,
As he comes to set everything right on earth,
Set everything right, treat everyone fair. (Ps 96:11–13 MSG)

Let it be so. Amen and amen.

Q & R

1. List some of the magical places you have treasured in your life.

2. When have you experienced deeper connection with God and yourself from being in nature? Think about each category of earth, sky, and water.

3. Return to the constellation you began drawing in chapter 1. Study it, add more star moments to it in light of subsequent chapters. Sit with it—are your unique patterns and themes beginning to take shape?

* * *

CHAPTER 14

Sensuality:
Becoming Comfortable
in Our Own Skin

I am going to say something that is atrocious for a married woman to say.

A guy who is not my husband put his arm around me in a club in Vegas . . . and it felt good.

We were celebrating Cameron's bachelorette party, and some of the women I was with made friends with a group of guys who were there for a bachelor party. We were sitting in a booth all together, and one of the dudes put his arm around my shoulder. It lasted for maybe a minute until I shifted out from under his arm and made my way to the dance floor. It was a minute that awoke memories of first dates and first touches. He smelled of a different cologne than the one worn by the man I have slept with for fifteen years, an awesome man whom I adore and find extremely hot even after all these years.

Still, having another man touch my shoulder in an endearing way was nicer than I wanted to admit.

I thought about the experience for nearly a week after I got home from Vegas. I couldn't get it out of my head. It bothered me. Feeling good felt dark—dirty even. Why was it so nice to have a man put his arm around me? I didn't say anything to my friends because of shame. Shame that I had done something inappropriate simply by having feelings.

I processed for a few days and came to realize that there are all sorts of experiences that feel nice. Eating a decadent meal, taking a hot shower, holding my babies against my bare skin. All these very physical things make my body feel alive. And that is good. Experiencing goodness with our skin makes life richer and more beautiful.

So why did I feel so much shame? I didn't reciprocate that man's affection; in fact, I ran from it straight to the dance floor. What if it just came down to the fact that I was uncomfortable feeling good? Why couldn't I simply acknowledge this moment as a compliment and move on without any emotional investment or shame?

Many of us who have a spiritual frame of reference have misperceptions about the story God tells us about our bodies. The story starts with the idea that we were created by a good God. This God is a craftsman who, when he is finished creating, looks at his work and declares it good. Another part of the story is that humanity's earliest experiences were in a garden. A garden named Eden, which in Hebrew means "delight." The story goes that these first people were naked in a garden named Delight, with delicious food growing all around them. It is interesting to me that the original design for humanity was to live with our skin exposed to the world, unashamed of our bodies, and enjoying good things that grow wild, and the place that delivered all these opportunities was called "Delight."

As the story unfolds, we read that the desire for knowledge and power got the better of these first humans. They wanted insider knowledge of great and unsearchable things, but little did they know that what they would learn wasn't life-giving but rather life-taking. In their quest to know God's mind, they learned they were naked, and they became ashamed. They were so aware of their vulnerabilities that they lost the ability to enjoy all that Delight had once offered them.

Ultimately, they were banished from the garden. The curse they carried with them as they left was that their work would become all-consuming. Basic provision for their bodies would burden. The land would grow thorns and thistles that would complicate their efforts. Clearing thorns and tilling the ground would fill their days.

Delight was forgotten.

Fast forward a lot of years, and a man who is God in skin gives his life in exchange for the curse of being banished from the garden. A crown of thorns is placed upon his head as a symbol that thorns no longer have to be a burden. The kingdom is being restored; delight returns. He has come that we might have life and have it to the full. The only issue is that we have yet to remember what it feels like to delight.

Over the past few years since that night in Vegas, I have been thinking about what it means to delight. To regain a sense of Eden on my skin. Because living fully means calling things good, feeling unashamed of our bodies, and feasting on good things that grow wild.

In *Women Who Run with the Wolves*, Dr. Clarissa Pinkola Estés tells a story from a Kiché tribeswoman who explains that she'd worn her first pair of shoes when she was twenty years old and still wasn't used to walking with what she described as "blindfolds on her feet."[1] Reading this, I couldn't help but think about how we blindfold our senses.

---

1   Clarissa Pinkola Estés, *Women Who Run with the Wolves* (New York: Ballantine Books, 1996), 24.

We wear layers of clothing to separate ourselves from the climate.

We isolate ourselves from our neighbors behind fences and locked doors.

We package our food in plastic bags and metal tins and send it so far from its origin that we forget where it came from.

We shy away from making eye contact with strangers, let alone engaging in deep conversations with them.

And rarely do we let our skin touch the world around us.

What would it look like to regain intimacy with our environment? How would our daily existence feel different if we stopped to feel the warm sun on our face? What if we splashed in puddles instead of walking around them? Would our delight increase if we breathed in deeply when we walked out into the fresh morning air, or if we allowed ourselves to be awed by a sunset, even though we have seen the sun disappear beyond the same horizon a thousand times before?

This becoming aware of our skin and senses means being sensual. There are so many connotations about this word that relate only to sexuality, but I would argue that sensuality is simply taking pleasure in our senses. Remembering that we are beings who have skin and eyes and ears and smell and taste. All our senses are meant to give us clues about the world around us, meant to help us taste and see that God is good.

For many of us, owning our sensuality means coming home to our bodies. For centuries, faith traditions have been uncomfortable with bodies. In fact, for many of us in the West, our spirituality is esteemed for being self-contained, prudent, and internal. This translates into spiritual practices that teach (intentionally or not) that being holy means denying our skin. An interesting result of this type of thinking is that sometimes religious people are dry, boring, and hard to be around. It doesn't have to be this way.

While I understand there is great benefit in learning to control our appetites, I also believe that there must be ample time for delighting. Just as there is a subtle dance of sunlight and moonlight in a day, there must also be a healthy mix of fasting and delighting. There must be time for less. For less eating, less having, less spending. And in those moments of fasting, we learn we can survive on less of everything and still be okay. But there must also be time for feasting. And this isn't a time for moderation. It is a time for laughing too loudly and eating decadent foods and making love. In fact, I believe our view of what is spiritual is far too small and, frankly, far too boring. Dialogue can be as spiritual as silence, dancing can be as spiritual as kneeling, and feasting can be as spiritual as fasting. I also believe that a passionate kiss can double as a prayer.

Maybe today is the day to confront the beliefs holding us back from delighting in our environment and in our senses, because living fully requires confronting the thoughts that are life-taking rather than life-giving.

One of my obstacles is fear. The truth is, I have been in a relationship with fear for most of my life. Conditioned to hold my breath, waiting for something bad to happen. Scared that the goodness could be taken away any minute. My tangled thinking tells me that if I invest too deeply in enjoying, then I will feel extra terrible when it doesn't last. My go-to tactic was to numb everything, to stuff any dark feelings that made me feel afraid, and to minimize delight so I would never have to be disappointed.

The process of starting to numb happens slowly over time. We get hurt or embarrassed, so we intentionally protect ourselves from pain. But we also keep good things out. We become so afraid of the dark that we forget to enjoy the light.

Another thing that keeps us from delight and sensuality is control. When we let our hair down and feel good things, we sometimes start to think we are being too much, too out of control, laughing too loudly, indulging too extravagantly. Or we diminish our delight so we appear in control or don't embarrass ourselves.

But here is the truth: There is no prize for the most composed.

Delight rarely happens when we are collected, controlled, and living in our heads. Delight isn't complete until it's expressed. I love people who can be free with their delight. They hug longer than everyone else. They sing louder and cry more freely. They tell everyone around them just how much they love them and never worry about looking like they are in control. They are free to feast and to enjoy their sexuality. Sensuality has become comfortable for them, and because of that they enjoy life more than the rest of us do. Perhaps they understand holiness as it should be. When we find freedom in our delight, we remember a sacred and wise part of ourselves, a sensuality that our bodies were created to enjoy. It is an acknowledgment that God's kingdom is being restored.

So what might this look like in your life? It would be presumptuous of me to tell you what delighting looks like for you, but I have some ideas that might spark your thinking.

One of my friends decided she was going to worry less about herself. She made a pact with herself to stop waiting around for other people to meet her physical and emotional needs. Instead of feeling disappointed that she wasn't being romanced or taken care of or appreciated like she wished, she started focusing on becoming those things for other people. She put all her effort into becoming a loving mom, an epic lover for her husband, a healer of bodies (she works in natural medicine), and a giving friend. After a few months, she suddenly realized that when she focused on making others feel good, she had all the things she was offering to her world. Sometimes sensuality is achieved when we offer it to others first.

Another idea is to ask, "When was the last time I let myself experience everything?" Do you even remember? Sometimes it is helpful to analyze how present we are in our lives. Because living through things—just getting by—isn't really living. We can live through the day or we can choose to really feel and delight in all the moments that compose a day. This has everything to do with paying attention. The next time you eat, let your taste buds overwhelm you; let your mouth feel the texture. The next time you hear your favorite song, let the music move you. When you snuggle a kid, smell their hair and kiss the soft skin on their forehead. Let your senses delight in the unnoticed pleasures all around you.

Maybe it is time to reawaken a sleeping part of yourself. Are there activities that make you feel alive? For my friend Di, it is cooking a beautiful meal. My friend Jackie feels alive when she is performing on stage. Is there an activity you have shelved because it felt impractical or because there wasn't space in your overcrowded life? Occasionally making space for the impractical but life-giving does wonders to restore a sense of delight.

Finally, remember your sexuality. I am not just talking about sex. Sexuality is so much more than intercourse. It has to do with creative energy that invites us to heightened awareness of the beauty and pleasure our body can enjoy. Get in touch with your feminine energy that has the ability to entice, to arouse. Become comfortable in your skin. Write your body a love note, thanking it for all the amazing things it senses every day.

Friends, we were made to delight. Let's resist the urge to take life so seriously. Let's push against the impulse to be in control all the time. Today is the day to regain delight. This is holy work, so let's run at it with all our heart, soul, mind, and skin.

Q & R

1. What words would you use to describe how you view your body? Would you say the theme of these words is compassion or shame?

2. Which of the following obstacles to living fully do you relate to: fear, numbness, avoidance, self-protection, overcontrol, or something other?

3. What do you think it might look like for you to regain that sense of Eden's delight in your life?

* * *

CHAPTER 15

Feminine Power:
What I Will Teach My Girls
about Being a Woman

I was at the library the other day, perusing the children's section of literature, and came upon a book that informed my adolescence: *Are You There God? It's Me, Margaret* by Judy Blume. The book talks about all the super important things young girls are thinking about, including getting their first period. As I looked at the cover and thumbed through the pages, I realized that one of the most important ways I can help my girls navigate their own transitions in life is to give their rites of passage dignity. To talk about things openly, to share my experiences, and to give them books like Judy Blume's to help them know that everything they are experiencing is normal and something to be celebrated. Here are some words I will share with my girls when the time comes on what I have learned along the way about being a woman.

To My Daughters,
  My period surprised me today—not unlike almost every month since I was twelve. I have never been able to calculate how many days to expect between starts. My body is not predictable like so many of my friends, who know down to the hour. It's quite possible you'll get my unpredictable genes.

But you're little now, and your biggest concern today was if you could wear your mermaid costume into the bathtub. In a few years, you will be ushered into the tribe of womanhood, like all of us girls before you. And just like for the rest of us, the process will feel confusing and thrilling all at the same time.

I don't know what it was about experiencing milestones that embarrassed me so much. When I wore my first bra to school in sixth grade, I was convinced the whole world could see my bra straps under my shirt. I felt like I was exposing my deepest secrets to the world and shouting, "I'm getting boobs!" to anyone who looked at me.

And then, my period. Even though I was fairly well educated about what to expect, when I actually did get my first period I was completely undone. Up until that point, the sight of blood meant that something was not as it should be. Seeing red also meant that something significant was happening—whether I was ready for it or not. (I have to tell you there have been a few times since that first sight of blood when I have literally cried tears of joy at seeing my period arrive . . . but those are stories for another time.)

In other societies throughout the world, getting your first period is considered so special that it is commemorated with special rituals and celebrations. I, however, haven't quite figured out a way to give dignity to getting your period. My friends and I have been trying to figure out how to honor you when you get your first period, but I know that pretty much the last thing I would have wanted my mom to do when I got my period was to commemorate it with a group of her friends, holding hands and cheering me into fertility. I promise to try to keep it classy for you.

When you get your first period, well-meaning people will try to tell you that you are woman now—which will no doubt make you feel weird (says my twelve-year-old self). I promise to resist this temptation, because the truth is you are becoming a woman, but you aren't one yet. Menstruating doesn't automatically make you a woman. Time mixed with hard choices, responsibility, and one or two really bad decisions to cut your own bangs will be a few components that string together to form your individual journey toward becoming a woman. Becoming is a process, and as far as I can tell, we never fully arrive. Our whole lifetime is meant to be a wonderful opportunity to try, risk, make some mistakes, and celebrate the journey of striving to become the most whole version of ourselves.

As you grow into your femininity, you will realize that you are gaining a new sense of feminine power. Power to entice and excite, to fill your world with creative, life-giving energy. You will discover that you have the ability to light up the world with your presence. You will notice that when you listen well, it makes people feel known and valued. You will learn that you can change the energy in a room and that your hug can change the trajectory of someone's day.

With all this beauty and creative energy you bring to the world, you will be noticed, and when you are, you will learn that your body has tremendous power. This is where you will have to make some choices—choices that I desperately want to make for you, but that are yours alone to decide.

Here is the thing: Your body is a gift to enjoy. A gift for you to offer. It is going to be tempting to share your body with men you meet along the way, because it seems like the most natural expression of love you can offer someone. Let me tell you from experience. Sharing your body with a man with whom you have no commitment has the potential to wound you. From what I can tell, the most fulfilling way to enjoy your body is to find a man whom you decide is worthy of your future, and then choose to commit your whole self to him. The physical pleasure your body is capable of is holy and good; don't let anyone convince you otherwise.

I am absolutely certain you will make mistakes along the way. Please don't be too hard on yourself. The consuming love of God that formed you is always there to restore you.

One last thing about bodies. Too often as women, we do battle with our bodies—trying to make them fit a certain ideal, wrestling with food issues to conform to impossible standards. If I could offer you any advice, it is to learn how to enjoy yourself. Many of the most beautiful women I know are stunning, not because they have the most symmetrical faces or toned thighs, but because they like themselves.

They enjoy good food and laugh unashamedly; they don't feel the need to obsess over every blemish; they have decided they are beautiful, and because of that, everyone believes them.

Girls, this whole process of experiencing "firsts" is an invitation for you to experience the world in new ways. At some points, it may feel like your body is betraying you—but it isn't. It is offering you new opportunities to experience the life-giving power gifted us as women.

So, my beauties, ask me anything. Nothing is off limits. I am by no means perfect at this being-a-woman business, but I have learned some things by making a few mistakes and will be glad to share all about them when you are ready to hear them. May you enter each new season of life with grace and excitement rather than shame. May you find a new sense of dignity with each milestone. I love you desperately and wholly. You are going to grow into the most wonderful women, whom I can't wait to call friends.

All my love always,

m

Q & R

1. What would your twelve-year-old self have loved to hear from this letter about womanhood?

2. Take a quiet moment to check in on how you view your period, fertility, sexuality, and body image. What perspective shift is needed to feel more positive ownership of the woman you are?

3. What do you hope to model to your children, boys or girls, about being a woman?

* * *

The Light over the Dinner Table:
Cultivating a Hospitable Heart

I have had to get over my house. I live in a teeny-tiny house. It is cozy and messy. My kids love art projects, which means that there is sure to be glitter in my carpets. This makes me pause before inviting people over. It also means that if we waited to have a perfectly spotless house before people could come over, no one would ever cross the threshold of our home. Ever.

When my kids were little, it felt exhausting to invite people over. The thought of having to clean my house and do even one more dish seemed like just about the worst idea I ever had. What I realized, though, is if I wanted to raise kids who know how to be warm hosts in their own homes, I needed to model it. Cue the exhaustion. Seriously, another lesson I had to model? Couldn't I just read them a book about it?

Here is what I did. I decided to take back the dinner party. In order to get over my fears that my house would never be clean enough or my culinary skills weren't up to par, I decided I would play out my biggest fear. So I called some trusted friends (ones who had kids; they are my people, they get it) and invited them over for dinner. Right now. No time to clean, no time to make any-thing fancy. Just right now. And because they love me and know I can be a little impulsive, they said yes. I had zero time to consult Pinterest to find out what the necessary essentials were for hosting a dinner party. In fact, I barely had time to change out of the purple sweatpants I had been living in for two days straight (don't you envy my husband?). Between brushing my hair and making sure all the underwear were off the floor, the only time left for culinary genius allowed for taking leftover lasagna out of the fridge to heat up. Yes, I served three-day-old leftovers to my friends for dinner. And you know what? It was one of the best dinner parties I have ever thrown. I didn't have time to stress about making every detail perfect. I wasn't running around like a mad woman, yelling at my kids to shove their toys under the bed. I actually enjoyed myself.

Since then, our family has been intentional to practice offering light to the people around us, so our kids see that showing hospi-tality in general is not as big of a deal as I once thought it was. For example, instead of having a garage sale, we are having a garage giveaway. We are putting all our extra stuff out on the front yard with a sign that says, "Take what you need." We want to be bet-ter sharers, and the truth is we have stuff that other people need. Giving it away is an excellent family-share opportunity and a wor-thy swap for the few bucks we would've made.

We also try to be more like my friend Jen. She has a knack for turning people who have no blood relation to her into fam-ily. She knows every neighbor's name, and drops off cookies just because. Just being around her makes you feel more like yourself. I am working on having a more hospitable heart, especially with the people who live next door and on my street and who share the pickup lane at school.

And when I get over my house enough to actually invite people over for dinner, here are some of the things we do.

We make simple food. I know, Giada De Laurentiis wants us to believe it's all about the food, but it's not. When we have guests over, I either make a simple dinner or order takeout (gasp!). I believe hot dogs can communicate love just as well as filet mignon, and I am more concerned about being together than spending hours in the kitchen, which isn't my thing.

We invite guests to help out. I purposely ask guests to help with small things when they arrive. It gives them something to do rather than just standing around, and the truth is, people like to participate. An all-hands-on-deck mentality ups the comfort level for everyone. Also, I like knowing that our friends know where to find things in my kitchen. There is something about witnessing another person's junk drawer that bonds you for life.

We ask good questions. One of the best ways to connect with friends is to ask great questions. I love to ask questions that help me learn more about their lives and how they feel about things. Everyone appreciates when someone makes the effort to learn unique things about them, because real security comes from a feeling of interconnectedness, of being IN IT with people. Asking questions and really listening to the answers removes barriers and makes people feel at home.

I like to have people think I keep my house immaculately clean, but the truth is, I don't. So I remind myself about the times I have enjoyed myself the most at a friend's house. Was it the biggest or nicest house, and were they gourmet cooks? Nope. What made me love being there the most was that I felt loved. This gives me the confidence to pack out my tiny house, serve the leftover lasagna, and love my neighbors like crazy, even if I have dog hair all over my couch. Deep breaths help a little, too.

So don't worry if you can't cook or your house isn't as fancy pants as someone else's. The mantra at our house is that it's more important to do it wrong than not at all. So invite people over, heat up some leftovers, and don't worry about perfection. Some of the most brilliantly blinding experiences of goodness I have enjoyed have included sitting on the floor and eating day-old pizza with people who love and celebrate with ease.

And if for some reason the dog eats all the hot dogs off the counter, or your kids bring a snake they just caught into the house to show you and it accidentally gets loose—In. Your. House.—just consider it entertainment and get on with the show. Everyone loves a good snake-in-the-house story, and you just gifted them with one to share.

Q & R

1. What are your fears about hospitality?

2. What are your favorite memories of being hosted in someone's home? What specific elements made you feel good about being there?

3. What do you want to teach your kids about hospitality?

4. Boldly name your next hospitality growth step! (It can be a baby one.)

* * *

CHAPTER 17

The Bus Stop:
Things Are Always More than Meet the Eye

Last night I couldn't fall asleep, so I asked Joe to tell me a story as we lay in bed next to each other. He, of course, went the route of a funny story about how we should have sex. No surprises there.

Joe is the person I get to share a lifetime of epic adventures with. The one who stays awake with me when I can't sleep, and who knows all my stories and believes the best version of every single one. You know that a story is good when there are multiple ways of telling it, and every version has a deeper meaning than you thought.

That is why I want to tell you three stories about a bus stop, each one a glimpse into how darkness and light weave tales that leave us wondering where one ends and the other begins.

THE BUS STOP THAT WASN'T

Not long ago, I was listening to a podcast called Radiolab. It is a thought-provoking show on NPR that is described by a producer as Miracle-Gro for the mind. On this particular day, they shared a story about an innovative approach to caring for patients with dementia and Alzheimer's. The story begins in a facility called Benrath Senior Center in Düsseldorf, Germany. The nursing home, which cares for many elderly people with dementia, had a problem many such facilities face: patients with dementia frequently become disoriented and confused about where they are. One man believed he needed to get to the local university because he was expected to teach a class (earlier in his life he had lectured at that university), while another woman believed she was a child and needed to get home to her parents, who were waiting for her. In most situations, patients experience extreme emotional duress when the staff attempts to reason with them. Many senior centers have experienced the very scary moment of not knowing where a patient is because they have "escaped" in search of their alternate reality. When this happens, the home has no choice but to put the patient on lockdown for their own protection. Sad but true.

This is where a man named Mr. Goebel comes in. Mr. Goebel, a member of the board of the Benrath Senior Center, presented an unconventional solution, which at first made everyone laugh. His idea was to build a bus stop in front of the nursing home. His thinking was that in many of the wandering incidences, the first thing many of the dementia patients did was look for public transportation. Therefore, if there was a bus stop right out front, the chances were good that a staff person would find them before they were in any real danger. The only catch with this bus stop is that a bus would never come.

At first, the leaders of the senior center thought it was a ridiculous, even borderline cruel idea. But as they considered the situation, they all agreed that trying to reason with the patients was much more traumatic. The bus stop might actually be a gentle way to let them sit with their confusion until it passed.

So they built it.

The next time the patient who believed she was a child became desperate to get home to her parents, she began to panic and cry, and every effort that the nurses made to try to calm her only escalated the situation. Changing their approach, they let her go outside to the bus stop. The woman sat in fresh air under a shining sun, waiting for the bus. A short while later, a nurse came out to wait with her. They sat side by side, and eventually the woman forgot why she was there. They went inside together for a cup of tea. It was a gentle way of letting her navigate her reality with dignity instead of frustration.

Now when a patient is missing, the staff will almost always find them sitting at the bus stop. When the patient arrives at the stop, the mood is dark and urgent, but after a while the urgency disappears and calm returns. Patients find equilibrium at a bus stop that isn't a bus stop.[1]

Things are always more than meet the eye.

A BUS DEPOT NAMED GOLGOTHA

In Israel, there is a city-bus parking lot that sits on the outskirts of the city. In this parking lot, buses that serve the Arab community line up at night after the city lights have dimmed and the collective breathing of the people has slowed. Bus drivers pull in, park their seven-ton buses, and leave for the night, often walking past a large hill of dust and stone. This hill has an eerie resemblance to a skull, which has been naturally carved into the rock by years of weathering. Local legend says that, while this piece of land is currently the site of a bus depot paved with concrete and soaking in diesel fuel, at one time it held a collection of three wooden poles dug deep in blood-soaked dirt.

---

1   Lulu Miller, "The Bus Stop," *Radiolab*, 23 March 2010, http://www.radiolab.org/story/91948-the-bus-stop/.

Thousands of years ago, this same ground was the spot where light and dark kissed. Three men were brought to this dusty landscape to meet a brutal death. The crowd that came to witness the events of the day huddled together, a mixture of friends and enemies. The accusers waited with eager expectation; the faithful in guttural disbelief that this one, the long-hoped-for Restorer of the kingdom, was being hammered to a tree.

As soldiers cursed at the crowd to get back, this one's hands were stretched as far as east is from west—open, exposed, an offering to the world that it didn't know it needed. And then, as metal pierced bone, his flesh became a statement about the flesh of each of our own hearts.

As the criminals hung, the stench of warm blood and the sweat of flesh perspiring from pain and fear were carried on the gusts of wind that picked up dust from the ground. As the crowd watched these three men gasping and groaning, as they counted their remaining breaths, the onlookers' collective respirations became tentative and erratic. Watching another human die is never comfortable.

The minutes became hours, as the morning light yielded to a puzzling midday darkness. Then the One, who was light to some and darkness to others, mustered a breath and shouted, "God! Why have you deserted me?"

The desperation was palpable to everyone.

And then this God-man, quietly resigning to his waning breath, whispered, "It is complete. Father, into your hands I commit my spirit."

He exhaled and it was finished.

On the same dirt where this man, who shook the world with his ideas about love and sacrifice, offered all of himself for the sake of humanity, a sea of parked city buses sit.

Things are always more than meet the eye.

CHARLOTTE AND BAILEY

In our family we like to do cool and scary stuff with our kids, like rock climbing and hiking mountains. We have developed a mantra we say to one another: "You have strong bones and you are brave." We know that the words we speak over each other matter, so when one of us is climbing the side of a mountain and becomes scared, we remind that person that they've got this, that they have strong bones and are brave. It is a little inside family mantra that has meaning for all five of us.

Charlotte is the youngest member of our family. At seven, she is the life of the party, funny and feisty and always ready to have fun. On school day mornings, she walks to the bus stop where, without fail, ten-year-old Bailey is waiting. Bailey attends the same school as Charlotte and always gets to the bus stop early, probably to get out of his house sooner. He is in third grade and knows more about life than most twenty-year-olds. He cusses and wrestles hard with his brothers. He also likes to pick on the littler kids, Charlotte included. Charlotte can't stand Bailey. He is rough and mean, and if she had a choice she would not be within fifty feet of him at any time.

But then Monday happened.

Charlotte and I were waiting for the bus, just like every other morning, while Bailey and his brothers passed the time with full-contact wrestling. One of the older siblings got angry and punched Bailey so hard that his nose began to bleed. Bailey sat down on the curb and started sobbing into his sleeve.

Before I could even process what was going on, Charlotte walked over to Bailey, sat down next to him, put her hand on his shoulder, and in the purest act of compassion and bravery said, "You have strong bones and you are brave. Did you know that?"

Even bus stops can be filled with unexpected compassion.

But it isn't just the bus stop. It seems to me that there is always something bigger at work. A story that is woven throughout space and time, connecting my story and your story in a way that will one day make perfect sense. Because all the space between you and me, and our nearest bus stop and the hill that looks like a skull is somehow connected, and our job as humans is simply to notice it. To bless the space between with as much compassion and gratitude and patience as we possibly can. Because the more we see, the more mysterious and connected the universe becomes.

So next time we get agitated or disoriented, maybe we can remember that sitting in the sunshine might help us regain our equilibrium.

Perhaps when we feel deserted, we can choose to believe that God has the last word.

Or maybe the greatest gift we can offer today is to put our arm around someone who makes us uncomfortable and to offer them words of hope.

Because who knew that a bus depot would be the place where our souls are healed.

And a fight at the bus stop would remind us that we are brave.

Because a bus stop is always way more than it appears to be.

When light and darkness kiss, everything becomes infused with holy, healing power. May we all have eyes to see that, even when darkness comes during the day, there are good stories ahead. Stories woven through space and time with bright strands of redemption.

Q & R

1. In what situation in your life are you hungry to find the deeper meaning?

2. How would you be enriched by viewing the world as more interconnected than perhaps you currently do?

3. As a small but important part of the whole big story of
   life, what do you want your contribution to be? Do you
   hope to embody compassion, gratitude, and patience
   in your little corner of the world?

* * *

CHAPTER 18

The Power of Story:
Illuminating Meaning
for One Another

About a year ago, I was sitting at a car-repair shop, waiting for the oil to be changed in my car. All three of my kids were with me, and I was fully engaged in entertaining them with silly games and conversation. It was taking forever for my car to be finished, so I had to pull out all the stops to keep three littles from running wild in the waiting area. As the kids and I talked, had balancing contests, scrounged through my purse for random stickers, and I-spied every animal in the pile of magazines lying on the coffee table, I noticed that a man, who was sitting across the row of chairs from us, was watching our every move. At first I projected that he was judging me for the noise we were making, but as I peeked up to get a more accurate vibe on the situation, I realized that he wanted to talk. He kept trying to make eye contact with me, looking for an opportunity to start a conversation.

At this point in the oil change adventure, I was literally sweating from all the physical and mental energy I was employing to keep my kiddos happy, and I had no resources available to offer this man who was looking for small talk. Seriously, could he not see I was busy wrangling three little souls?

But he persisted. His first question was innocuous, "Aren't kids the best? I love how much energy they have." He was trying to offer me some perspective that all was well, that he was paying attention to the events of the morning and was enjoying taking it all in.

I responded with a quick, "You are so right," still not really interested in opening the door to further conversation.

"I wish my kids were still little," he responded.

And with this statement, a man to whom I had spoken a single sentence began to share his story with me. Like a waterfall being held back by a dam about to crack, his eyes filled with tears and he spilled.

He told me about his three kids. They were grown now with families of their own, but they never made time to visit him. I learned that he had been an airline pilot who was more committed to raising his rank than his kids, which meant he was never home long enough to build a deep connection with anyone. He encouraged me not to sacrifice relationships for anything else in life, because he had and regretted it immensely. Life was lonely, and he needed to say it out loud.

It was then that I felt the need to be near him. To be close enough to offer my presence in a way that says, "I hear you. Your story is changing me." So I switched chairs to the one to his right.

His tears stopped, and he said matter-of-factly, "I am dying. I probably have a month to live. So I am spending my last days taking care of all the little details, like getting oil changes in my car, so my kids don't have to deal with any of it once I am gone. I hope that it will in some way be a peace offering for the details I missed when they were young."

At that moment, the man behind the counter called out his name. He grabbed a cane that was propped up on his left side, which I had somehow missed noticing earlier, and he gingerly stood up. Grabbing my hand, he looked me in the eye and said, "Thank you for listening. You are a great mom. Pay attention to the details and life will mean more." Then he kissed the back of my hand before hobbling to the counter to pay.

For a moment time stood still.

I could barely believe I had almost missed the opportunity to share a few moments with this man, who offered words that were now branded onto my soul and kissed onto my hand.

Listen, notice the details, and it will all mean more.

When was the last time you truly listened to someone? *Really* listened with the express purpose of bearing witness to their story? When was the last time you sat with someone and felt truly seen and heard?

There is something about listening and being heard that fulfills a deep-seated human need for connection. Instead of needing to be fixed, most of the time those who tell us their stories just need to be loved. And it goes both ways: the experience of telling someone vivid stories about our life changes us, and it also changes the perspective of the listener.

I love listening to a good story. Everyone has the relative who is the storyteller at the family gathering. The one everyone gravitates toward to hear them recount tales of family history and recite hilarious inside jokes. I was born into an entire family of storytellers. As a kid, I couldn't get enough of our family stories: a bubble gum cake where the icing turned into something that resembled chewing gum; my large family spending summers jam-packed into a small house near the beach. I knew that my great grandma had gotten pregnant out of wedlock, which was a huge heartbreak to my grandad's pastor father. I heard how Grandad left England in order to make a better life in the United States, and how Nana and her baby crossed an ocean all alone when she was only eighteen years old. I heard tales of how they made a new life and could hardly breathe because they missed their families so much. How they sacrificed and worked hard and loved each other fiercely. The stories drew me in and made me feel part of something bigger—a circle of love that extended beyond me and gave me inside information on our collective story, and how it had shaped me. Good stories are important in that way.

Throughout history, passing down stories through an oral tradition has shaped our human narrative. Whole groups of people learned about their identity through the storytelling of their elders. Stories served as guides through the darkness, beacons of light offering perspective when the future felt shaky. Hearing about how our collective history has been shaped by victories and defeats, we realize this is our story, too.

Listening and sharing ignite embers of hope, because stories highlight our resilience. That is why at our house every night before bedtime, we all snuggle in our bed, and Joe and I tell a family story. We have learned that providing opportunities for kids to listen to our family stories is one way to develop resilient kids.

Marshall Duke, a psychologist at Emory University, was asked to research stress and resiliency in children. His research found that kids who know a lot about their families tend to do better when they face challenges. Dr. Duke developed something called the "Do You Know?" scale that asked children to answer twenty questions. Examples included: "Do you know where your grandparents grew up?" "Do you know where your mom and dad went to high school?" "Do you know where your parents met?" "Do you know an illness or something really terrible that happened in your family?" "Do you know the story of your birth?" The study concluded that the more children knew about their family's history, the stronger their sense of control over their own lives and the higher their self-esteem. The "Do You Know?" scale turned out to be the best single predictor of children's emotional health and happiness well into adulthood.[1]

1   Kara Powell, "How Much Your Kids Know about Your Family Narrative Matters," *Fuller Youth Institute*, 1 April 2013, https://fulleryouthinstitute.org/blog/how-much-your-kids-know-about-your-family-narrative-matters.

I have learned that the most helpful family story is the oscillating narrative that goes something like this: "We've had ups and downs in our family. We built a family business. Your grandfather was a pillar of the community. But we also had setbacks. You had an uncle who was once arrested. We had a house burn down. Your father lost a job. But no matter what happened, we always stuck together as a family." Dr. Duke says that children who have the most self-confidence heading into adulthood are the ones who have a strong "intergenerational self." They know they belong to something bigger than themselves.

It is equally important that they feel heard, so they will tell us their stories as well. I love this quote by Catherine M. Wallace: "Listen earnestly to anything [your children] want to tell you, no matter what. If you don't listen eagerly to the little stuff when they are little, they won't tell you the big stuff when they are big, because to them all of it has always been big stuff."[2]

It seems to me that one of the greatest gifts we can give our kids is to look them in the eye and really listen. So often days go by, and I realize that I and my children have been circling around one another, eating meals and doing life near one another, but not really seeing each other. When we show our kids they are worthy of our attention, we gift them with a sense of value. And when they feel valuable, they are more likely to grow into adults who will extend that same gift to our grandchildren. It is a generational blessing.

It is holy, holy work, listening. I have come to consider it my life's work to listen deeply, because everyone I will ever meet knows something I don't. When we listen and learn from one another, we are participating in the holy. God's kingdom come.

It should come as no surprise to us that the original storyteller

---

2   "Listening to Children in Their Early Years," *YouTube*, 28 February 2014, http://www.youtube.com/watch?v=sprfqH-KFok.

is our Creator himself. In the Bible, the Lord is referred to as the Author of Life, who chooses to communicate through a compilation of stories and metaphors, so that we can recount our own stories in an equally compelling way.

One of my goals for this year, in addition to looking my kids in the eye and really listening to them, is to listen to the voice of the Storyteller, who is weaving together stories of my past and future so I can know to whom I belong. When I quiet my mind to take notice of the details all around me—the stories others are offering, the words of my kids, our family narrative—I hear the Author of Life speak personally to me in the listening. Sometimes what I hear isn't what I'd hoped for, but that only pushes me harder through the darkness to find the light of truth. Like in the car-repair shop. Darkness and light and listening offered a kiss on the hand and offered beautiful details that have made my life mean more.

Q & R

1. When was the last time you sat with someone and felt truly seen and heard?

2. When was the last time you truly listened to someone?

3. Make a list of family stories you want to pass on to your children.

4. How would you rate your own listening skills?

* * *

CHAPTER 19

The Eyes Have It:
Celebrating a Worthy Calling

Start a conversation with someone on an airplane, and without fail one of the first questions asked is what kind of work you do. Sometimes this question is answered in the heart-wrenching way I heard at a party last week. A friend of ours asked a woman he was meeting what she did for a living, and this woman's cheeks blushed as she sheepishly said, "Oh, I'm just a mom."

Just a mom.

I cannot tell you the number of times I have heard these same words used, whether by my friends or in my own head. But I have become convinced that being a mom is the bravest work we may ever give ourselves to. It requires the kind of courage that chooses to show up in the best ways we know how—to find our calling in the midst of our very real days. And it is the kind of work that will never reciprocate with material rewards or daily accolades.

To say that moms have a "work ethic" is like saying Niagara is a "waterfall." It's accurate, but it doesn't explain the force of what you are describing. But working hard is different than feeling like what you do on a daily basis is what you have been placed on this earth to do. I think this is why we resort to the "just a mom" response.

I think that what I and so many of my mom friends are often lacking is a sense of vocation—a highbrow word that comes from ancient Latin speakers, who called it *vocacio*, which literally means "a call or summons." It is the deep-seated knowledge that our current circumstances are part of our life's work. That what we have before us today and tomorrow are holy opportunities. That we were created with a purpose, and our destiny is to participate with God to write a good future.

For many of us, the tension lies in the fact that we are trying to cobble a sense of identity. We are wrestling with a desire to use our education or natural talents, or to pursue a career that will help us to feel like we are our best selves. And we are trying to do all this while facing the very real limitations that accompany the various seasons of motherhood.

What I need to remind myself of continually is that this mothering gig is a vocation. A calling toward holy work. I need to realize that all work is God's work, and there is profound meaning in the tasks right before me. In other words, even the mundane brings him glory. All the to-dos that accompany my vocation of motherhood matter to God.

I attended a kindergarten musical extravaganza last year that was just about the most precious experience I have ever had. My favorite part of the performance was when all the kids walked onto the stage, and I saw my daughter Charlotte standing in the second row on the right-hand side. As she took her place, she began to scan the crowd. Her eyes searched frantically until she met my gaze. Her eyes lit up, and she offered me an enthusiastic wave that said, "I see you!" A visible sigh of relief moved her small chest. I am her home base. Her focal point in times of uncertainty and doubt.

I am becoming more and more convinced that there is something about our eyes that is insanely important in reminding our kids who they are. Not only does making eye contact ground them and remind them they are seen, I believe that we remind their souls they are delighted in when our eyes light up to see them. Toni Morrison asks what makes our eyes light up; it seems to me that our kids are asking the same question. They are wondering, "Do your eyes light up when I walk in a room?" I love showing up to school and making eye contact with my kiddos as they come out the door to get picked up. You would think we haven't seen each other in five years by the way our eyes light up to see one another. This is something we have intentionally cultivated. I want my child to know that the very sight of her affirms that she is worthy and loved.

Being a mom means we are called. Called to raise generations. Called to be the brightest light that signals our kids toward wholeness. The world is holding its breath, hanging on our every word. Waiting for us to speak into existence love and hope within our children's souls. Every act of love we bestow, no matter how small, opens doors, dispels fears, and teaches our kids to love this way, too. Each day (whether we are ready or not) we harness the light and do the best we can. As moms, we learn compassion and empathy, and we become more courageous—reaching deep inside our hearts to do what needs to be done. Because that's what moms are called to do.

When you are a mom, it all matters.

Kissing that boo-boo and putting Band-Aids on, just because. That matters.

Watching your kids do the same trick over and over again on the trampoline and each time acting as if it was the most impressive trick you have ever seen. That matters.

Snuggling on the couch and telling stories in a silly voice. That matters.

Waking at dawn and kissing goodnight. That matters.

These holy moments matter to our kiddos, and they matter to the world. For the rest of history, echoes of our voices will be heard.

Sometimes we need to be reminded of this. Too often we are cruel to ourselves and tell ourselves things that aren't true. We lay awake at night, shaming ourselves for all the things we aren't, or haven't done. We wonder if anyone notices. We feel guilty when we wake up in the morning already looking forward to bedtime. We go through the day, thinking that if somehow we just fed our kids a little bit healthier or read one more story or were a little more patient, then we would be enough.

Just in case today is one of those days when you are wondering if what you are doing really matters . . .

Wondering if anyone notices,

if anything you are doing is world changing,

feeling like your shoulders are heavy with worry.

If you woke up today already looking forward to bedtime—

Here is your truth for the day:

Motherhood is your worthy calling for today—and you are significant. Just as a lighthouse beckons souls toward a safe harbor, the work of your day will woo your kids toward a light called home.

Q & R

1. Do you believe that your current circumstances are an important part of your life's work?

2. How do you think moms should answer the party question, "So what do you do for a living?"

3. How would you benefit from believing all work is God's work, no matter how mundane?

4. Do you truly believe that the daily acts of mothering weave together a whole that is far greater than the sum of all those tiny daily activities?

* * *

CHAPTER 20

To Live like Music:
Learning to Feel All
Our Feelings

I think I may have had a small mid-thirty life crisis this morning. That, or I was reeling because the dog ate my favorite pair of ankle boots.

Those are the only reasons I can think of for this morning's breakdown on the way to kid drop-off at school. An old Counting Crows song came on, and suddenly it was fifteen years ago, and I was on a train somewhere between San Luis Obispo and San Diego, headphones on, sitting next to Drea and choking back tears over a boy who wasn't good for me anyway. Now it's a thousand Wednesdays from that day, and I'm listening to Counting Crows sing over the speakers in my car, while two little girls, who look just like me, sit in the back seat. And I remember exactly how it felt to be on that train, and how I am the same girl who cries at songs, only I don't have scrunchies in the bottom of my backpack.

Music has the capacity to stir deep delight. It can also make sorrow sound beautiful. When we hear lyrics that remind us of a moment, what if we paused to feel them?

Let me tell you about the kind of music my grandpa makes. If you ever meet him, you will recognize him right away by his

Hollywood smile and voracious appetite for life. He is the one dancing under the stars to big-band music on the top floor of the bath house by the lake or traveling the world by cruise ship. Please don't remind him that he is eighty-seven and should be thinking about slowing down. He would never have time for that.

My grandpa is a renaissance man, who worked at Kodak for thirty-five years. In his spare time, he raised three kids, was a devoted husband, built his own home, served in the military, and picked up more hobbies than me and all my friends combined.

One of those hobbies is writing and starring in musicals. He works for a year on each show, crafting scripts and weaving his favorite songs throughout. Then he gathers a ragtag group of people from his church to star in it. They are the ones who don't get asked to star in plays. Most of them have shaky voices. They come from a humble community of hardworking people, and many are retired and living on fixed incomes. They are gentle with one another, cheer for one another even when someone messes up, and allow each other to shine in the most beautiful ways possible. They practice for a few months in Grandpa's family room and then put on a one-night-only performance in the basement of his church. My grandpa has the gift of being himself and inviting everyone around to join him. He makes the world better just by being in it. And he writes beautiful plays that help us all to believe we have a song to offer the world.

Not too long ago, the adorable Ellie and I flew to New York to be there for what he said was going to be his last show. My mom also flew in, and because she arrived a few days before us, she got a singing part in the performance. She had only a few days to pre-pare, and my grandpa, being the consummate professional that he is, made sure she practiced the song to within an inch of its life. Mostly because it was a duet with him, and he was going to make sure it dazzled.

For this particular show, Grandpa envisioned a dinner-theater vibe. And when Grandpa has a vision, the family rallies to make it happen. So my aunts and uncles and cousins cooked meatloaf and chicken in the basement kitchen of the church, and I joined in cutting onions and washing forks. But really, my relatives are the holy ones—the ones who show up and cook food and serve meals to messy people. And as I sat there chopping and washing, I felt like I could burst with love for these selfless people for whom nothing is too big a deal, because they are family.

At six o'clock in the evening, the show started. My grandpa opened, using his karaoke machine as a microphone, and he and my mom sang. I cried. The show continued with my fearless aunt, who sings even though she feels like she can't. She was followed by a sixty-year-old woman who had never sung in public. The acting was endearing, but it was the music that moved me. I had never heard music like it. And it had nothing to do with what was being sung. It was the sense of inherent worth that each person performing was given through their moment in the spotlight.

After each performance, the audience cheered like they were clamoring for Bono to sing an encore. The audience was made up of equally beautiful souls, with bodies shaking from Parkinson's and hunched over with osteoporosis. These are friends and neighbors of my grandpa who have never missed a show and shower him with praise when the final bow is taken.

And the whole time the play was going on, my Ellie was being bombarded with love from our family. They included her in preparing food and serving drinks. They told her how beautiful she is and how they couldn't have done any of this without her. They validated her just for showing up and included her just because she is theirs. And this middle-born child, who is intuitive and sensitive and feisty, hugged me around my waist and said this was the best place she had ever visited. This child has traveled the world, yet in a basement surrounded by family is where she would rather be. And I wanted to hug her for a hundred years. I wanted to hold her and surround her with love and happiness from now until forever. I wanted her to know that this is the real stuff. The true stuff.

The evening was so packed with goodness that I could hardly breathe.

Music has the potential to move us in unexpected and healing ways. For our anniversary last summer, Joe took me to a Train concert at Red Rocks, an outdoor amphitheater in the foothills of the Rocky Mountains. The rocks that jut up from the ground and surround the stage make for a world-renowned concert experience. As the sun set, and the stars became visible, Train played the song "Calling All Angels," the crowd raised their hands to the sky, and it was the best church service I have ever been a part of. Joe and I kept looking at each other like "this is so cool." We sang and clapped, and the lights of the stage partnered with the stars to create the best light show I have ever seen. I felt alive in a way I hadn't in a long time.

There are so many gifts in opening our hearts to the melodies that surround us. Music carries hope and truth when we have nowhere else to look. Even when dark feelings occasionally come—just like dark lyrics—they are simply opportunities to feel deeply. Like I do at my grandpa's plays.

My kids love it when I sing to them at night. I don't have a great voice, but they don't care. They also don't care what song I sing; they just love that I am with them and they have a few more minutes before they have to go to sleep. Often after I have sung, and we are sitting together in the dark, they spill their guts. Things they have wanted to share come out in the dark. Hurt feelings, frustrations, questions—it is as if a safe space has opened up, and they can unburden their minds before falling asleep.

The Bible uses all sorts of imagery to help us understand God. Warrior, nursing mother, pregnant rock, mother bird, and I am compelled to argue—singing mom.[1] There is an obscure part of the Bible written by the prophet Zephaniah, where we read about God singing a lullaby. "For the LORD your God is living among you. He is a mighty savior. He will take delight in you with gladness. With his love, he will calm all your fears. He will rejoice over you with joyful songs" (Zeph 3:17 NLT).

I know that we translate it with a male pronoun, but I can't help but wonder if this is actually God acting like a mother, singing a lullaby. Could it be that God, who compares himself to a nursing mom, might also be telling us that God's nature is maternal, and offers us lullabies to calm us so we can sleep? Three o'clock in the morning is usually when I wake up and worry about all the things I have no control over. I don't think I'm alone. I talk with women all over the world, and so many of them tell me they can't sleep either. Maybe we need to ask our singing Mother for a lullaby so we can unburden our hearts and minds. Maybe we need God to sing a freedom song over us, declaring that we are no longer trapped or oppressed. A song that relieves us of the things we shouldn't be carrying, so that the darkness no longer frightens us.

May we all learn to live like music. To be okay with all our emotions. To make them all worth feeling. May we listen closely for the songs God is singing over us. And may we raise our hands under the music of the night sky and say to the friend sitting close to us, "This is so cool."

---

1   Lauren F. Winner, *Wearing God: Clothing, Laughter, Fire, and Other Overlooked Ways of Meeting God* (San Francisco: HarperOne, 2015), 25. There is a phenomenal chapter about gender and language for God that I highly recommend, plus I love everything Lauren writes.

Q & R

1. What are your inspiring songs? What is it about them that transports, transforms, or relieves you?

2. As you think about "feeling all the feelings," does this strike you as negative or positive? Why?

3. How can you make space to unburden your heart and mind before bed the way children do?

* * *

CHAPTER 21

Failing Gloriously:
Redefining Success
and Failure

All these things have been said by members of my family in the past month:

"Mom, the only question you helped me with on my math paper is the one I got wrong." She is in first grade, people.

"My mom says bad words sometimes, too." (Spoken to the lady in the grocery store who just let loose an expletive, followed by, "Why aren't there any ripe avocados?" and who then was embarrassed when she realized kids were around.)

"Mom, why does the candy from Santa have T.J. Maxx tags on it?"

"Really, the tooth fairy is running late again? Our tooth fairy is a total loser." (Said by me.)

"Mom, I am just going to sleep in my clothes because then I don't have to get up as early." My reply? "Sounds like a great idea."

And these are just the things I am willing to put in print.

Sometimes I feel like a total failure as a mom. To be honest, it doesn't take much to convince myself that I am letting the entire world down because of my failures both big and small. And it doesn't just apply to mothering. I can tell you in great detail what I haven't done and where I'm failing in every other area of my life as well. It's how my mind works. I am a firstborn overachiever. My identity has always been linked in a very unhealthy way to accomplishment. For me, failure has always felt like the ultimate betrayal of my perfectionistic self.

Like most people, I have never enjoyed discussing my failures. I would recognize them and feel what is probably an excessive amount of guilt over them, but then I preferred to hold my shame in and chastise myself for not being able to avoid failure entirely.

That is, until I had kids.

It was then that I got to console my toddler who fell down when he was trying to take a wobbly first step, or my fourth grader who lost his class election, or my five-year-old who made her friend cry. The words I spoke over them in those moments sounded like this: "You are still awesome. This failure doesn't define you. Get up and try again. Say you are sorry. Make amends and then get back to playing."

All these words were so different than the taunting words I offered my own soul when I experienced failure. In a sense, motherhood gave me new eyes to see that failure can be the very thing that saves us.

This is what I've come to believe about failure: it is good.

Just like childbirth is good. And by good, I mean incredibly painful. My first baby showed up after thirty-seven hours of labor, thanks to a very intuitive nurse who told me that I needed to stop fighting the pain and work with it instead. Failure hurts, but there is tremendous potential for goodness to be born through it.

Which is why a few years ago, after a particularly big mistake, I decided to become really great at failure. To give it a new name and bestow it with fresh meaning. So I made a pact with myself and wrote down four things I would do when the shadows of failure threatened to block out the sun.

Here is my pact:

I will tell everybody. As much as my go-to behavior is going to be to hide, I give myself permission to fail publicly. I will not pretend that I can hold it all together so no one feels sorry for me. When I mess up, or my husband's business implodes, or the one brave thing I have been giving all my efforts to doesn't happen the way I planned, I will let other people in on it. I will share my shame because the world is healthier, and my soul is healthier, when I do. My friend Shauna Niequist says it like this in her book *Bittersweet*: "This is where our insides open up and we are delivered right into the palm of God's hand, which is where we wanted to be all along, except that we were too busy pushing and pulling our life into exactly what we thought it should be."[1]

I will pity party. I think it is important to feel my feelings, for a little while. This means I will feel the blow, curse, sob, and throw myself a pity-themed party. But as soon as the party is over, I will begin the work of pulling my weary bones up off the ground and of shining light into the wreckage. Failure has the capacity to show me who I've become, in the worst ways, and also in the best ways. When things fall apart, the process of sorting through my broken pieces will be the most perilous and precious chance I get to come home to myself. Because of this, I will choose to find shimmers of light in the shadows and will become masterful at learning whatever I can from the experience, so that my failure doesn't go to waste.

I will remember Myshkin. It seems to me that so much of the guilt and shame we experience around failure is a result of our misunderstanding of what success is. One of my favorite TED talks is by a guy named Myshkin Ingawale. Myshkin is a scientist who used his talk to explain how he was driven to create technology that would help test for anemia, because people were dying

---

1   Shauna Niequist, *Bittersweet* (Grand Rapids: Zondervan, 2013), 8.

unnecessarily. He said, "I saw this need. So you know what I did? I made it." The entire audience burst into deafening applause. And then he said, "But it didn't work. And then I made it thirty-two more times, and then it worked."[2] When I think back to my greatest successes, they have all come on the heels of my greatest failures. It seems to me that success is simply getting up and trying again. And again. And again.

I will remind myself that life is lived in the both. I will resist the temptation to label an experience either a success or a failure. I will remember that it is always both. Because life isn't success OR failure, it is success AND failure. I will remember that my friendships, my education, my marriage, my parenting have all featured wins and losses, ups and downs, highlights and lowlights. Light is just as much a part of an eclipse as is the shadow. I will choose to embrace both the light and the darkness in every experience.

It seems to me if we want to do brave things and influence the people around us and maybe even the world, at some point we are going to fail. We are going to stumble. We are going to fall flat on our face. These are vital parts of our journey. Failure has the capacity to show us who we're becoming—in the worst ways, and also in the best ways. When things fall apart, the process of sorting through our broken pieces will be the most dangerous and precious chance we get to come home to ourselves.

We are best to interlock fingers with the failure and welcome its wisdom.

So here's to our most undignified, glorious failures and to the innovations of the heart that come from bringing them into the light.

---

2   "A 20 Second Blood Test Without Bleeding: Myshkin Ingawale & Laura Espiau at TEDxGateway," *TEDx*, 11 February 2013, http://tedxtalks.ted.com/video/A-20-Second -Blood-Test-Without.

Q & R

1. How do you define failure?

2. How has motherhood changed your view of failure?

3. What lessons have you learned from failures? Do you think that only failure could have taught you these things?

* * *

CHAPTER 22

Banishing Our Ghosts:
Confronting the Shame
That Holds Us Captive

Her closet smelled like hairspray and tobacco, which made sense; even after only having known her for ten minutes, I could tell that these were two of her favorite things. She sat in the kitchen, barely ninety pounds, gray hair teased into a bun that sat neatly on the top of her head with not a hair out of place. Her long, graceful fingers were gently tapping ashes from the end of her Marlboro lights. She was paying me to organize her closet and to help get her house ready to sell, but instead of sorting through the piles of treasures she had accumulated over the course of fifty years, she asked if I wanted to sit and join her for some iced tea. She placed two ice cubes in a glass, added a slice of lemon, and then with two shaky hands lifted the pitcher and gingerly filled my cup. We talked for two hours before I actually got to work. During those two hours, I learned a lot about her life, but it wasn't until I sorted through her closet that I really got to know her.

Inside the four walls of my new friend's closet was a lifetime of treasures and painful memories. Tucked into a box in the back, I found a newspaper clipping that revealed she had competed in the Olympics. Three wedding rings from her three husbands spoke volumes, as did the FedEx envelope stuffed to overflowing with foreclosure warning letters from her mortgage company. Sitting on top of an old movie projector were photo albums filled with thirty years' worth of Christmas memories with her kids. Next to the photo albums, neatly folded in a plastic bag, was a blanket her mom had knit for her first baby. It was almost too much to take in—the love and sorrow, accomplishments and secrets, all shoved into the cracks and crevices of her most private spaces.

I have a secret fascination with closets. When I was in college, I made extra money by organizing the intimate spaces that hold all the paraphernalia that compose a life. You can tell a lot about a person by the things they choose to store in the nooks and crannies of their closets. Secrets and memories hidden in shoe boxes and shoved in between sweaters; boxes of letters from past lovers; locks of hair from a dear one who passed; pairs of what-is-this-anyway giant underwear, the kind that are so comfortable but that you wouldn't want anyone to know you actually wear. Often our closets are where our most treasured possessions, as well as the things we want to hide, reside.

Hiding secrets and treasures in our closet usually starts when we are young, and often our childhood collections end up in our adult closets. At least this is true for me. Boxes of ticket stubs and pictures from prom; dried flowers; the green sweater I wore to my first day of kindergarten; a pair of cleats I haven't worn in years. In addition to my childhood treasures are a few things I work hard to conceal, including some boudoir photos I had taken for Joe for our tenth anniversary, a Costco supply of condoms, and a secret stash of chocolate, all of which I want to make sure my kids don't see.

When we were kids, my brother Charley's closet contained an assortment of dirty laundry, a wooden sword that he got at a Renaissance festival, smelly football gear, an assortment of G.I. Joes, and a stash of cash that he was always saving up. One year, our dog decided to give birth to eight puppies in his closet. Not wanting to disturb the new mom, he decided that they could consider his personal space their home until their eyes opened and they grew big enough to venture out into the world.

As far as I can tell, no one is immune to having weird stuff in their closets. And it isn't just our physical closets, is it? It is the inner spaces of our hearts and minds, the psychological closets that hold our fears and memories and secrets.

When Charley was really little, he believed that two ghosts lived in his closet. They had names and distinct personalities and were so terrifying that the mere thought of them kept him up at night. As adults, we often have our own ghosts. They lurk in the darkness of our mind, holding us captive to the shameful secrets we never want to expose to the light of day. All of us have said things we aren't proud of; we've all been wounded, felt insecure, and done things we're embarrassed about. We have worn-out ideas that we choose to hold on to, shame that we don't process, wounds that we aren't willing to expose to the light. Usually our go-to response is to get rid of the uncomfortable feelings as quickly as possible. We mobilize every resource we have to navigate the situation, but often we succumb to the terrors of what we try to keep hidden.

This is when our ghosts are born. And we believe that if anyone finds out about them, the response will be too painful to bear. So we shove it all into the back corners of our inner spaces and try to forget. As time goes by, we get better and better at stuffing our brokenness, whether it is by medicating to numb the voices of our ghosts or running from anything that scares us. As we shove more secrets and shame into our closets, we live smaller and less free.

I can't tell you how many nights I have spent trying to outrun the things that made me uncomfortable. I also can't tell you how many years I have spent pretending I don't have any ghosts that need to be confronted. It is easy to pretend we don't have ghosts—until we can't any longer. When we can't breathe deeply anymore, when we feel worn out from trying to keep things hidden, the longing to live free becomes more compelling than the fear of facing our ghosts or disappointing people.

I believe that confronting our ghosts begins with asking ourselves some questions. Questions like: What would make me feel humiliated if anyone found out? What are the addictions, the fears, the past wounds I need to own up to? What are the insecurities and secrets that need exposure and release? What is weighing me down right now, and how would my life be different if I was free of it?

I started to see a counselor this year. I was noticing some patterns in my life that I was willing to admit were holding me back. At my first appointment, one of the first things Michal, my therapist, shared with me was that so many people feel shame about looking into their own darkness. It is not uncommon to project that God feels about us how we feel about ourselves. We believe that the terrible things we think about ourselves are the same thoughts God has about us. But it isn't true. Regardless, it is this kind of thinking that makes it hard to peek into our closets.

Confronting our ghosts is hard. W. B. Yeats wrote, "It takes more courage to examine the dark corners of your own soul than it does for a soldier to fight on a battlefield." But however hard it is, it is made all the harder in the avoiding. Avoiding just keeps the issue in circuitous motion; it comes back around every so often to see if we are ready to deal with it. It never leaves; it just keeps rearing its ugly ghost head.

Alice at the Right Motherhood blog says it like this:

> But I do believe that we are all here with something specific to learn in our ever-onward quest to be the best we can be, heading toward that ever-elusive enlightenment, following our path. And each of us is born into this life with specific challenges to overcome and learn before we can take the next step, climb the next ladder-rung. But I should make even that a little clearer. It's

all about energies, really. You'll be born into a particular type of family, with a particular type of energy, in order to figure it out. And in not figuring it out, you'll carry it with you into the world, where you will attract more people and situations who will challenge you to figure it out. And in avoiding those people and situations, you'll encounter yet more who will challenge you to figure it out. Keep avoiding, keep encountering. Until you figure it out. And it isn't going to be easy. In fact, shining that light into that dusty old corner will probably be one of the hardest things you've ever had to do, because you will find your own ego there, staring back at you, and you will have to face it, and then let it go.[1]

There are four things I have learned so far from wrestling with my ghosts and cleaning out my mental closets. First, it is in hitting rock bottom and becoming desperate enough to do something different that things start to get better. There is total freedom in "losing it all" and discovering that the only thing you ever needed cannot be lost.

Second, no one can do my work for me. As much as I wanted Michal to give me answers, they weren't hers to give. She was there to help me discover what needed to be healed. The scary work of shining light into the darkness was up to me.

Third, the moment I stopped caring about what other people thought about me was the moment I started to heal. The truth is, we don't need to be liked or loved by everyone all the time. In fact, if we are, we probably weren't being ourselves anyway. For me, this meant I had to invite people into my closets and be honest about what I had been keeping secret. This was an act of congruency for me, of pulling together all the divided parts of myself and working to become whole again, comfortable being my true self in every situation.

---

1   Alice, "A Light in the Darkness," *Right Motherhood*, 15 February 2013, https://right-motherhood.wordpress.com/2013/02/15/a-light-in-the-darkness/.

Lastly, in order to live without shame and fear of exposure, my light had to shine bright—first inward to face my darkness, and then outward for the world to see. Once we turn the light on in our own closet, we can share that light with the people around us. When we find freedom from the fear and shame that haunt us, we are called to help others who are dealing with the same ghosts get free as well. My friends and I call this repurposing our closets. This helps us remember that our hard-won healing, which always takes longer than we thought it would, can be used to help others heal their own broken places. The scars we wear on our backs and hearts from evicting our ghosts are given purpose when we expose them to others with similar wounds. Kicking out our ghosts gives others the courage to evict theirs.

I like people who know their ghosts. The ones who have waged battle with their fears and come out the other side a little freer and a lot more compassionate. They are the beautiful ones who go through life reminding others that they are not broken beyond repair. That all our wounds can be redeemed, and our battles with our ghosts can point others toward healing.

My friend Emerson spent four years of his life in federal prison for dealing drugs across the US and Mexico border. Now he is an artist who takes found industrial garbage and makes breathtaking installations on Hollywood Boulevard. For a lot of years, he didn't talk about his past because he was embarrassed and thought his mistakes were a liability. That is, until a few years ago when he shared his story with his faith community, and people in the audience were so moved by his courage that they, too, found the nerve to face the ghosts in their own jail cells, if you will.

Another woman named Sara emailed me a few weeks ago to share a story of knowing her ghosts. She is a MOPS leader who had secrets that she was terrified to share with her group. Her story was that early in her twenties, she had a series of relationships in which she chose to have two abortions and was feeling terrified of being judged for those decisions. She was now married to a great guy but was tired of holding her breath, waiting for her secrets to be revealed. She volunteered to open her closets and share the stories that she had packed away in fear. As she revealed her shame to the hundreds of other woman in a group she led, three women came up to her afterward to share their own ghosts that have the same name as Sara's. She freed other women from their ghosts because she was brave enough to talk about her own.

Here is the deal: we were created to live free and unashamed. God tells us that the thief (our ghosts) comes to steal, kill, and destroy, but Jesus has come that we might have life to the full (John 10:10). Full to the brim with deep breaths, open hands, and organized closets.

Maybe today is the day to fling open the closet doors, in order to begin the holy work of confronting your ghosts.

May we all find the courage to confront our ghosts. May we feel the relief of banishing anything that is weighing us down, and may we shine a light on our shame so that we experience freedom and cleansing in unexpected ways that bring wholeness and health to our inner spaces.

Q & R

1. What is weighing you down right now? How would your life be different if you were free from it?

2. Are you tempted to avoid instead of facing the dark corners of yourself? What are a few of your favorite avoidance strategies?

3. How do you feel about this quote? "Each of us is born into this life with specific challenges to overcome and learn before we can take the next step." What are your specific challenges? How far have you come in surmounting them? What do you believe is your next small or big step?

4. How do you feel about letting your safe friends see inside your closets?

5. What would be an "act of congruence" for you? That is, what is one action that would begin to pull together disconnected or hidden parts of your true self? (For example, being more honest, asking for help, confessing something, taking a new risk, etc.)

6. Can you dream of how you and your life would look if you lived free and unashamed?

✳ ✳ ✳

CHAPTER 23

Confessionals:
Finding the Courage
to Be Honest

Have you ever sat around a bonfire pit under a sky of stars and realized how magical a campfire can be? There is just something about being huddled around a common source of warmth and light. Sometimes we are so mesmerized by the crackling and flickering that we feel compelled to sit quietly as we take it all in. Other times we fill the air with raucous laughter, as we struggle to find our breath amidst the goodness of being with friends.

We have a bonfire pit in our backyard that we call the confessional. When people are over and end up sitting around the campfire, we are known to break out the wine, and people start saying things they have been holding in.

I am not immune to spilling stories around a fire. One Memorial Day a few years ago, we were sitting around a fire in my brother and sister-in-law's backyard, talking about things we regretted. Most of the stories revolved around drinking too much or not making it to the bathroom in time. That is when I told a story that my brother insisted I never repeat again. Ever. He says it is going to make you think horrible thoughts about me. But I am all about full disclosure, so here is the dirty truth. During college, I dated four different guys at the same time. And they didn't know about each other. I was the bad guy (girl) in a not-so-romantic comedy that didn't have a happy ending.

The short version is that I had just broken up with a long-term boyfriend, and for whatever reason, four different guys asked me out on dates within a few weeks of each other. Because they were each so different, and let's be honest here, totally good looking, I decided to go out with each one. It all started out very innocently, but as the weeks went by, I found myself falling for each guy for different reasons. The problem was, I was getting scared that they were going to find out about one another. My roommate had to cover for me, and I was sneaking around to avoid getting caught. I had created a tangled mess.

I was being untrue to each of these guys—and of course the story ended horribly. I was out with one guy when I ran into another one of the guys. There was a messy confrontation, and instead of having four great guys to date, I ended up with zero.

At the end of the whole ordeal, my heart was broken, and my head was just barely inhabitable. I thought such awful thoughts that I cannot even say them out loud. I was humiliated and embarrassed that I hadn't been honest sooner—like from the beginning.

Have you ever been scared to be honest, or done something that put you in a situation where you dreaded being found out? You know you need to confess, but the words feel too heavy to speak out loud. But when you muster a moment of courage that allows you to speak your secrets, they suddenly seem so much less powerful. To me, being honest feels like I have been holding my breath for a long time and finally get to inhale. The longer I hold on to an untruth, the more desperate I am to breathe.

A fact about being a human, who lives under sunlight and moonlight, is that each of us does unhealthy things to feel centered and whole. More often than not, we experience shame about those things, and then the shame causes us to shove it all under our mattress to try to pretend it isn't there. But it is. And it is making it hard to sleep. The more we have hidden, the harder it is to share our lives with other people, which is just the kind of connection we crave.

Do you ever feel overwhelmed by shame? Or maybe yours is more like a low-grade, nagging shame that surfaces when you least expect it. One friend said it felt like the light-darkness mix in her soul had become a swirling hurricane, and what she didn't know until recently was that saying what it was out loud was the only way to defuse its Category 5 power.

Saying it out loud.

Maybe that is the answer.

Joe and I work hard to make truth telling easy in our family, because honesty is a high priority to us. I don't want my kids to carry around anything they don't have to. I would rather hear the truth about what they are feeling or doing than have them think that there are secrets that need to be hidden, because they are too dirty or shameful to be shared. I am a firm believer that secrets make us sick.

At our house, every topic is open for discussion. My kids ask questions about sex and injustice and are keenly interested in discussing cuss words and why we shouldn't use them. Yesterday in the car, my daughter shared with me about the two times that she lied at school in kindergarten two years ago. I think she needed to get it off of her chest.

Here's what's hard. Truth telling is embarrassing. It exposes our guts to the world and to our friends and to our spouses and, sometimes, even to our children. Early in my marriage, I was embarrassed to tell Joe what I needed because I didn't want to be perceived as needy or demanding. But he missed out on being my partner in the ways I needed most, simply because he didn't know what I needed.

Hiding from the truth causes us to feel alone and can turn the hairline fractures in our lives into deep, gaping chasms. Often when this happens, we end up filling in the gaps with things that don't serve us well. There was a point in my life where I filled in my gaps with exercise. Other times it was with sleep or overcommitment. Busyness is another way I keep myself from confronting the real issues that need my attention.

Here is another truth. For so long I felt like I had to manage my relationships. I would coach Joe on how he talked about his job, worried that he would be perceived a certain way. I worried about what people would think, or how they would judge the unconventional decisions we made. I was my own full-time PR person, and it was exhausting.

Whether we are managing other people's perceptions of us or hiding things because of shame, our secrets hold us captive. So in an effort to live unencumbered, every once in a while I will ask myself, "Do I have anything going on in my life that no one knows about?" And if I do, then it might be time to get honest with someone.

In Catholic traditions, confession is incorporated into the rhythm of spiritual practice. I think they are on to something. Their ritual is to go to their place of worship and to say out loud the things that are weighing on their soul. The things that they have done or said or experienced and feel are holding them back from being the best version of themselves. The most important part of the equation is that they say it to another person.

In my Protestant faith tradition, we are told to confess to God and all will be forgiven. And while I appreciate this straight-to-God's-ear tactic, I can't help but feel that it is incomplete. Not in the sense that God needs more, but in the way that I need more. I need to say it out loud, to get it out of the darkness so that it can't hide in the shadows any longer. Some of my friends are working on convincing their faith communities to install some type of confessional in their church buildings, because we all need to say it out loud in order to calm the hurricane-force shame in our souls.

I believe in truth telling because honesty is medicinal. It has healing qualities that neutralize the fears that make us sick. When we speak secrets out loud, it breaks their power over us. It also allows other people to become free from their own secrets.

I asked a friend of mine, who is a Catholic priest, what the trick to confession is. He, in a very holy way, told me that this was a weird question. And then he answered it anyway. What he said is that the "trick" to confession is being specific. So many people enter his confessional and confess to generally bad things like envy or lying. But he says that he prefers to think of confession like going to the doctor. You may be embarrassed to mention a specific ailment, but if all you can offer the doctor is an "I don't feel well," then he can't do much with that. When you say out loud, "This is my wound," the door opens to healing. We can either say, "I need healing (generally)," and maybe we'll get it . . . generally. But how much more do we need specific healing—and being specific about our pain is how we unlock the door to that.

Another friend of mine counsels women who have trauma from past abortions. She told me that almost one hundred percent of the time, the women she works with experience tremendous healing in naming the baby they aborted. It is as if giving a name and saying it out loud brings some resolution to the painful feelings that they have kept buried for years. When we are able to name the things that live within us, even if for a short time, we face our inner darkness and bring our shame out into the light.

In the past month, I've had to get really honest with my closest friends, also known as the priests in my life. We are talking ugly honest. When they see the most unsavory truths about me and continue to show up in spite of it, I am reminded that trusted friends help make everything better. The only thing worse than struggling is struggling in secrecy. So often we think we are the only one. The only one who has struggled in marriage or in parenting. The only one who doesn't like a kid right now. The only one who is thinking horrible thoughts toward someone and doesn't really want to stop.

I have relied too heavily on niceness for most of my life, which means that I have had the tendency to round off the edges. When I say hard things in the nicest, non-emotion-evoking way possible, the words often end up meaning nothing at all. And there's nothing nice about that—it's just a form of hiding. My need to have everyone love me had convinced me that I couldn't be honest. But that didn't serve anyone well. The people who I loved most never got my whole self. They got nice Mandy, but they often missed out on the real me. I valued honesty so much from everyone around me, desperately wanting to know their honest truths, but I wasn't willing to offer myself to others in that way. So I am working on being more direct and confrontational when appropriate.

Becoming a mom has helped me tremendously, because it has given me the courage to use my voice. When I had kids, suddenly I was free to express my needs in a new way because I was advocating for the needs of my babies. I wasn't afraid to ask for what they needed from doctors, from teachers, or from strangers at the playground. I knew what I wanted and was able to ask for it because I was advocating for them. No conversation was too scary when it was for the good of my children. Now I realize that I have gained the same freedom to advocate for myself by asking for what I need, saying no, having hard conversations, or confessing the things that I have done and feel like hiding.

When I do, I often hear the response, "Me too." Rob Bell writes:

> Anne Lamott says that the most powerful sermon in the world is two words: "Me too." Me too. When you're struggling, when you are hurting, wounded, limping, doubting, questioning, barely hanging on, moments away from another relapse,

and somebody can identify with you—someone knows the temptations that are at your door, somebody has felt the pain that you are feeling, when someone can look you in the eyes and say, "Me too," and actually mean it—it can save you. When you aren't judged, or lectured, or looked down upon, but somebody demonstrates that they get it, that they know what it's like, that you aren't alone, that's "me too."[1]

Confessing to our friends and asking them to advise and pray frees us. I have never once regretted confessing to my loved ones about anything. On the contrary, they make me stronger, healthier, kinder, better.

Every. Time.

Because it is in the eyes of people who love us that we come to know ourselves.

Last night we held a confessional in our backyard. It smelled like burning wood and tasted like roasted marshmallows and melting chocolate, but it had the feel of a sacred space filled with warmth and light. It reminded me that making room for confession in our lives can take on the taste and texture of everyday practices. So let's create safe spaces where we can be truth tellers. Places where whole is more valuable than pretty. Where honesty is prized more than comfort. And let's be families that don't have to posture or hide, but allow one another to spill our guts so that we are free to live transparently and loved. What a gift it is to be able to remind one another that we were meant to enjoy our life, not be drowned by it. Huddled around a common source of heat and light, we can all find healing, because light and warmth can both consume our fears and set ablaze our passions. When we become willing to speak out loud what we need and what we need to get rid of, then the light can do its work.

---

1   Rob Bell and Don Golden, *Jesus Wants to Save Christians: A Manifesto for the Church in Exile* (Grand Rapids: Zondervan, 2008), 151.

Q & R

1. Can you offer yourself compassion for your past regrets, knowing most of them were likely an attempt at wholeness?

2. How does it feel to think about confessing everything you regret to another person? Do you see the benefit?

3. How are you at tolerating the embarrassment that comes with gut-level sharing?

4. What are your signature coping mechanisms? Is it exercise, overbusyness, sleep, or food? Do you long to be free from practicing them excessively?

5. Do you believe in the power of specific honesty to cleanse away shame? Do you believe it's true for you and not just for others?

6. Take some time to put words to what you need to add to life and what you need to get rid of.

* * *

CHAPTER 24

Earmuffs and Bachelors:
Teaching My Kids about Hearing God

We live in Denver. In the winter, my kids refuse to wear jackets. My son likes to wear shorts to school (even when it is snowing)—because junior highers are cool like that. For a long time I fought it, practically holding him down and forcing him to put on gloves and earmuffs and a warm coat. I was worried about how other moms would judge me when my kid showed up in a snowstorm in shorts.

And then I decided it was his deal. His decision if he was going to be cold. His decision about how he wanted to feel on the way to school. And so I gave up, packed away the earmuffs and scarves, and filled his drawer with shorts.

I embraced it.

I know now that it is very unlikely you will ever invite me to speak at a parenting conference. This will be even truer when I tell you more of our reality.

We go to church with homeless people downtown and invite kids over who use bad words. We send our kids to public school, and I often have to break up fights between two brothers who meet

us at our bus stop and whose favorite word to yell at each other is
… well, I'll let your imagination run wild. I let my kids use knives
to cut veggies, and I had no sleep rules when we raised our babies.
Most nights we end up with four people and a dog in our bed,
because two of our three kids have snuck in during the middle of
the night. We take our kids on scary hikes and encourage them to
rock climb sheer cliffs, because they can.

And now, after all that, I am about to say something that may
make you really uncomfortable.

I have a problem with church.

Especially the way we teach kids at church.

It seems to me that so much of how the church messages kids
about a faith experience is focused on raising gentlemen and ladies
who are civilized rule followers. We do the same thing with God.
We try to round off the edges, to make God more palatable, pretty,
civilized.

I have friends who fiercely guard how much of the Bible they
share with their kids, because they are worried that some of the
stories are too violent or scary. Have you read the stories God has
offered us as his words to the world? Many of them are dark and
fierce and will make you blush. It is exactly the kind of content I try
to shield my kids from most of the time. But can I tell you that those
parts of the Bible are my kids' favorites? They love the breathtaking
unpredictability of a God who invites people who have messed up
big—bigger than people in our modern-day prison system—and
then uses them to slay giants and change the world.

The thing I love most about Jesus is that he had no patience for
domesticated religious types who were drowning in their own self-
righteousness. He had no patience for the ones who were blinded
by the light. He preferred to spend his time with those more familiar with darkness, the ones on the periphery who did things that
made other people uncomfortable.

It seems to me that if Jesus came to my house today, he would show up as the bachelor uncle. The one who arrives with extravagant gifts and feeds the kids chocolate before bed, despite my disapproval. He would look them in the eye and throw his head back in laughter about the joke they just made up, then give them bear hugs that squeeze all the air out of their lungs. He would tell them scary stories about the adventures he has had and the bad guys he has confronted. My kids would fight to sit next to him, not wanting to leave his side because they might miss something. Jesus would play in the backyard and encourage the kids to jump off a tree stump from a height that feels just scary enough. He would challenge them to risk more than is comfortable and to love as big as they can. They would learn to stand up to bullies and share their snacks with the kids who don't have enough.

But sadly, this isn't the Jesus most of us meet along the way. More often, the faith we pick up is full of rules and regulations. I can't tell you how many adults I have met who have shared stories with me about growing up afraid of messing up and disappointing God rather than being wooed by an extravagant and loving Creator. I have seen too many kids who are raised in Christian homes but who are indifferent to faith and disdainful of church. Sometimes this is the result of witnessing hypocrisy; other times, it is the result of nothing more than monotony and boredom. But most often I believe it results from their perception that the church has no words to speak into their darkness.

It seems we have lost our words about a God who makes us uncomfortable, the one who made light and darkness and who has some really jacked up people for friends. We raise our children in a cocoon of grayscale faith, then wonder why they run as far as they can to find a real adventure.

Religion is held together by rules and rituals. Following Jesus is fueled by passion and mission. Erwin McManus says, "If our children are going to walk away from Jesus, I want to raise them in a way that they understand that to walk away from Jesus is to walk away from a life of faith, adventure and risk, and to choose a life that, without Him, is boring, mundane and ordinary."[1]

I couldn't agree more.

My twelve-year-old had the opportunity to accompany my husband on a business trip to Israel this year. It was a two-week adventure, filled with all sorts of unique experiences, like riding bikes through the ancient city to visit bakeries making challah bread for Sabbath, praying at the Wailing Wall, and picking up a stone from the Elah Valley, where a young David defeated Goliath. For weeks after he got home, we would find him sneaking to stay up late to read the Bible. Instead of turning off his light at 9:00 p.m., which is bedtime, he would close his door to hide the light so that he could read the stories he heard about on his trip. Joe and I hadn't done anything to encourage him to read; he was simply captivated by the stories of God. He had experienced them firsthand and was so consumed that he had to know more.

As parents, I am a firm believer that what we do says more about what we believe than what we keep telling our kids about what we believe. Because of that, we don't do family Bible studies. I would rather have my kids see us doing things rather than talking about them. Instead, we read the words God wrote down, and when we hear something that sparks a question or compels us to act, we do it. We pick up and move, we give more than makes sense, we make cupcakes for our neighbor. Whenever someone in our family hears God whispering in their heart, we talk about it and do something about it.

I want my kids to follow the captivating voice of Jesus rather than the conforming voice of religion. The most compelling times

---

1   Erwin Raphael McManus, *Soul Cravings* (Nashville: Thomas Nelson, 2006), 145.

I have heard Jesus are when I needed to act big and do something that didn't make sense. I can only assume that it will be the same way for my kids. After all, I don't want them to be wearing earmuffs because they are too worried about what other people will think.

I want them to do what is good out of love instead of fear.

I want them to be more concerned about what God is *for* than what he is against.

I want them to be able to see the invisible and hear the inaudible, because their hearts know God.

I want them to know that God isn't afraid of the dark.

I desperately want this kind of faith and relationship with God for each of my three kids, but the fact is, I am not enough to make it happen. It is going to take a community of people surrounding each of my kids in every stage of their growing-up years to cheer them on toward adventurous faith. And so I am committed to surrounding them with people who are salty and deep and holy. People like my mom and Ryan.

My mom. My kids call her Nene, and she is one of the loveliest and most real people you will ever meet. There are so many things I appreciate about the way she raised us, but one of my favorites is a tradition she started on our birthdays. Each year, my mom writes a blessing for every member of our family on our birthday. It feels matriarchal and deep and biblical. We tease her sometimes because of how seriously she takes it, but we secretly love it. She signs each one with a photo of herself doing a handstand, reminding us that we shouldn't take ourselves too seriously. I have been compiling every blessing she has given to my kids in a book for each of them. My hope is that when I hand them their blessings when they turn eighteen, they will know that the prayers of generations surround them, intercede for them, and have gone before them every step of the way. That the prayers and blessings of Nene took on flesh and blood, were put into action, and transformed into wonderful memories.

And Ryan. Ryan is a friend from San Diego. He is single, handsome, and the most eligible bachelor you will ever meet. On Sundays we do church together. Ryan, my kids, Joe and I, and a few hundred other people all jam our bodies into a too-small warehouse in Barrio Logan. I like to think that my kids enjoy church because of what they learn there, but the real reason they even consider going is because of the donuts and their friend Ryan Sisson. Mention Ryan to my kids, and they will tell you that he smells good and likes to chase them through the chairs. After all the talking and singing and normal stuff of Sunday mornings, the fun starts when my kids go looking for Ryan. Regardless of who he is talking to, when Ryan makes eye contact with one of them, he will turn, run, and scoop up their little body, turn them upside down, and the game starts. It might be a rousing version of tag, hide and seek, or chase-Ryan-through-the-building. Whatever the game, Ryan makes my kids feel seen and reminds them that church is jam packed with adventures that take their breath away and leave them entirely consumed with laughter.

This following-Jesus thing feels like the greatest mystery we could ever commit to. A mystery so deep and true and unknown that we need other people to remind us that we don't have a spiritual life, we are a spiritual life. People who point us in the right direction without telling us what to see. This is why I am committed to surrounding my kids with people who are salty and deep and holy in ways that will help my kids treasure their faith and the people who formed it, as each of them sets out on their own journey one day.

On summer nights, the kids and I often take a blanket outside to our backyard. We choose the perfect spot and lay the blanket carefully between the lilac bushes and the large maple tree that drops its propeller seeds onto our foreheads. Then we lay on our backs, shoulder to shoulder, and look at the stars. The middle kid always spots the North Star, and the oldest hopes for a comet or something wild and unexpected, while the youngest applies her best efforts to making shapes out of the dots that fill the sky. "Look!" she will say, "I see a horse, or maybe it's a unicorn." And as we gaze at specks of light formed long years before my kids were born, I remember that the God who made universes also made each of my kiddos. Each is a spark of light that has been given brilliance so they can shine in the inky night. Each is uniquely meant to bring a glimmer of hope to a world that is afraid of the dark.

So shine on Joseph, Ellie, and Charlotte. May your days be filled with brilliant light, and your nights with astonishing wonder. May my frail attempts to introduce you to Jesus make you laugh because you have already journeyed with him. And may you always remember that you are loved more deeply than words can ever illuminate.

Q & R

1. Growing up, did your family promote religious conformity? What were your family values?

2. What is the difference you see between the conformity of religion and the captivating words of Jesus?

3. Who are the friends, leaders, or authors who help remind you that you don't just *have* a spiritual life but that you *are* a spiritual life?

* * *

CHAPTER 25

Forget-Me-Nots:
Hope Looks like Despair

We moved around a lot when I was young, so I never really had the opportunity to become attached to the houses we lived in or the neighbors next door. But there was one place that was my home base: a tiny brown house on Alpha Street. A house that breathed love into my soul. The carpet on the stairs is burnt orange, and I spent many afternoons sitting on a landing halfway up and looking at the swirling pattern of the carpet while adults talked and ate. I never really heard what was being said, but that was okay because I felt what was happening. I think that is the beauty of being a child. The words matter, but not nearly as much as the feeling does.

You know when you are getting close to the tiny brown house because you drive past the Char Pit and then up Lake Avenue. When you see the corner store, you know you are almost to Alpha Street and Grandma Joan and more love than one little girl could ever hold. In the summertime, my brother and I would stay with Grandma Joan in the little brown house for weeks at a time. We climbed trees in the front yard and walked to Lake Ontario. Our favorite thing to do was to run as fast as we could, jump, and then cannonball into the waves. We had contests to see who could make the biggest splash. Grandma would sit on the edge of the water, making designs in the sand with a feather and cheering us on.

Whenever we arrived at Grandma Joan's, she would be sitting out on the stairs by the front door, waiting for the moment we arrived. We would explode from the car, and she would meet us halfway down the walk, wrapping us in bear hugs. It was always as if she was seeing us for the first time, savoring the sight of us. Each time I thought my heart would burst wide open from all the love she hugged into us. It was quite a scene. Mrs. Beauchamp, who lived across the street, would peer out her window, wondering what all the commotion was about.

Inside, I would sit at the long, dark table and sip tea with too much sugar and pick cookies out of the Winnie the Pooh cookie jar. We talked and colored. She let me try on all her jewelry. But the best part was just being there, sharing space and breath with my grandma and her love.

At night, she'd tuck us into bed in the blue room. That is what we called it. It was a cozy room with navy-blue paint on the walls and a window seat that looked out over the street. Grandma Joan would kiss our foreheads and tell us stories about the great Garloo, who lived down the bathtub drain. She made up stories that left us believing anything was possible. We would beg her to tell us more, and she would oblige until our eyelids grew heavy. And then she would tiptoe out of the room, leaving the door open just a crack, so the light shone through enough that we would never feel scared.

Sometimes after she left the room, I would climb out of bed and up into the window seat, pressing my forehead against the cool glass. A streetlight shone into the darkness, and I remember feeling like the light was the most beautiful thing, and the whole world was filled with wonder.

Being with Grandma in the little brown house felt like I had all the warmth and light under one roof I could ever need.

Years flew by. My mom and dad moved our family to California. I went to college and met a boy. Grandma would fly out to visit us once a year, and every time she left I would cry. Because saying good-bye to warmth and light is always devastating.

When Joe and I got married in a friend's garden toward the end of spring, Grandma Joan was there. She helped pass out favors—seed packs stuffed with forget-me-not seeds we had written notes of thanks on to all our guests. One of my favorite pictures from that day is a family portrait where, if you look closely, you will see my grandma and me holding hands, our fingers laced together, a simple reminder of our secret bond.

Two years later, I traveled to spend a weekend at the brown house. Grandma Joan and I watched her first great grandson, my first baby, play with her jewelry on the carpet. We both knew it was our last visit. I fumbled for words, trying to speak back to her all the love she had given to me. Nothing felt adequate. Her pain started to return, and she suggested we go out to the backyard so the baby could get some fresh air, and Grandma Joan could distract herself. The three of us walked slowly out to the backyard. She made herself comfortable on a plastic chair, and I looked at the flower beds lining the edge of the garage. For nearly fifty years, she had dug her hands deep into the soil of these beds, taking great care to cultivate the life that surrounded her.

At the end of our visit, I kissed her cheek. Neither one of us was willing to say what was actually happening, so we told one another we would talk soon. I flew home, and she entered hospice.

Not too long ago, I decided I wasn't living up to my legacy. I needed more love in my life. And realizing that I can't force people to love me better, I decided to start loving them better. Feeling love extravagantly wasn't going to be enough for me anymore. I needed to express it. So my mantra became to think less and love more. I stopped worrying about how my every action was going to be perceived, and I gave myself permission to be extravagant, to bring light wherever I went.

Loving big takes courage. It shows up at the house of my friend whose life is in ruins because she cheated on her husband. It cleans her dishes and reminds her that Jesus isn't afraid of messes. It refuses to let the fact that my dad couldn't tell me he loved me keep me from telling the people I love just how crazy I am about them. It moves intentionally toward relationships instead of finding differences. It refuses to believe there isn't hope. And it leaves a door open just enough to let the light shine through so no one feels afraid.

I know this is possible because Grandma Joan showed me.

Eight months after my grandma died, my grandpa called my mom to tell her some interesting news. Apparently, all over the grass surrounding the little brown house, in the flower beds and even in the cracks between the bricks in the pathway, forget-me-not flowers had come into bloom. They covered the entire yard, and my grandpa said he couldn't believe his eyes. What none of us knew was that in the months between when Grandma Joan first found out she was sick and before she entered hospice care, she had spent time in the garden, planting seeds. Seeds she had brought home from my wedding.

It has been over a decade since Grandma Joan planted those seeds in the cracks and crevices all around her house. My mom texted me this morning that she had just talked to my grandpa, who told her that the forget-me-nots were starting to bloom yet again.

Love never fails.

When I think about my grandma out in the yard, planting flowers as a love note to all of us long after she was gone, I can't help but think about how sometimes hope looks like despair. How beauty and mess go hand in hand. The good can look like a sunrise or a dying grandma planting seeds in her yard. It is this very hope that saves us. The hope that light is brighter than any darkness life can throw at us, and that all our extravagant gestures of love will reverberate for years to come.

Q & R

1. Who are some of the special people in your life who have enveloped you with love?

2. Where in your life do you want to bring the light of extravagant love?

3. Where can you sow seeds of hope that can reverberate for years to come?

* * *

CHAPTER 26

A Dazzling Unfolding:
The Process of
Becoming Ourselves

I refuse to be shamed by this truth: I love *Dancing with the Stars*. There it is. I said it. I know this is not cool to admit. It would be much more hip to say that I count down the moments for *Broad City* or *Game of Thrones*, but instead I love the cheesy theatrics and sparkly costumes of a ballroom dancing show. I think one of the reasons I appreciate it so much is that I am constantly inspired by people doing what they are gifted at alongside people who are giving all their effort to learn something new. This also means that I choked back full sobs at Ellie's elementary-school choir performance—not because every single one of the fifty-five kids in the choir sang with all their hearts whether they nailed it or not, but because their teacher stood up with her back to the crowd and shook her booty along with the music and led those kids through eight songs with full choreography—and had a blast doing it. She was doing what she does best. I sat there thinking, "She is such a great teacher! And look at these other teachers being so awesome, sitting in the front row at seven o'clock at night, not because they have to but because they want to cheer on their students. These are the luckiest kids on earth! Their light is so bright it hurts my heart with goodness."

A few months ago, I sat on a knitted, thrift-store blanket on the sidelines of my six-year-old's soccer game. I take this blanket to every one of my kids' sporting events to remind myself that the process of becoming takes time. Just as this blanket was knit by hand, my kids are in a process of being knit together, of becoming who they uniquely are.

On this particular day, four girls from each team chased the ball from one side of the field to the other. Some of the girls were naturally talented, while others had to work at it. There was one little girl on the other team I couldn't keep my eyes off. She had pigtails with pink ribbons and thick-lensed glasses. The other girls sped past her anytime she even thought about trying for the ball, and each time the ball came in her direction, she looked as if she was terrified of kicking it.

And then she did.

About halfway through the game, the ball landed straight at her feet, so she swung her leg and kicked the ball. It wasn't spectacular, but she did it. And before I could blink, she raised her arms into the air and shouted loud enough for all the parents alongside the field to hear, "I am AWESOME!" She was proud of herself and didn't care who knew it. She received the loudest cheers of the day. For kicking the ball.

What would it look like if each of us embraced our awesomeness and became willing to spread it around?

I went to a meeting recently and noticed that every single woman in attendance looked the same. Same boots. Same words. Same jewelry. And something in my gut told me this was all wrong. The variety of the creation outside my window shouts to me that God doesn't value uniformity, but uniqueness. Throughout history, well-meaning religions have tried to make us all the same. But the thing I love most about Jesus is that he calls us to be different.

What if, just like the little girl at the soccer game or the teacher in front of the choir, we decided to celebrate how our unique qualities and abilities are unfolding?

As I am sitting here writing, my six-year-old is snuggled next me, her small feet resting on the side of my chair. She likes to sit close. I am always in awe of this little one: her humor, her ability to aggravate her siblings, her deep emotions and freedom to share them. Each day I learn something new about her. And I realize that the wonder that compels me to love her unfolding personality is the same wonder I can extend toward myself. I can marvel at who I am and who I am becoming. It doesn't matter if I don't have myself all figured out. That isn't one of the requirements for participating in God's story. In fact, as far as I can tell, he prefers the people who are still figuring it out—because they are the ones who are actively searching and listening.

How long has it been since you spent time considering who you are becoming? What it is you really love? That thing that feels sacred because you are unapologetically yourself when you do it. What are the things that make you cry? What makes you angry to the point of saying, "Someone should do something about that"? Could the answer be you? Woven into every soul is a unique fingerprint left there by the God who knit us together.

But knitting takes time.

Emily Dickinson wrote, "The Truth must dazzle gradually/or every man be blind." God does not show us our entire unfolding up front. If he did, we would be blinded by the immensity of our story, the beauty and pain and wild intricacies. The process of becoming ourselves takes a lifetime, so the suffocating pressure we place on ourselves to understand ourselves completely isn't helpful. The freedom to be ourselves isn't found in one "aha" moment. Instead, as we keep walking forward, we are invited to discover parts of our souls that have been waiting for their time to emerge.

When I am tempted to cheer too loudly or to yell at kids on the other team for playing too rough, my thrift-store blanket reminds me that this process of becoming is more about experiencing beautiful moments and less about winning. May we all be dazzled by a brilliant God who is always unfolding before us something bigger than ourselves. And may we have the freedom to throw our arms in the air as we realize: We. Are. Awesome.

Q & R

1. What do you love most about watching your children become who they are?

2. Do you have patience with the learning curve of becoming your true self?

3. Take a few minutes to think. What do you love, what makes you cry, what makes you angry?

4. What would your "cause" be if you had to choose one thing to become an advocate for?

5. Describe your style of dress. Do you feel permission to break from the norm?

6. Do you believe you are awesome? What would happen if you did?

* * *

CHAPTER 27

Starry Night:
When the Next Step
Is Uncertain

A full moon was looking at its reflection on the lake when we convened on the dock. Midsummer heat made sleeping impossible, so we left our cabins to see what amusement the night offered. The three of us had become fast friends; not knowing anyone else meant we naturally gravitated toward one another. Within days, inside jokes had developed that would bond us for the entire summer.

We were finishing college in different cities and had decided a summer job at a camp in the mountains sounded just about right. The next summer, real life would press in on us with grown-up decisions about jobs. New responsibilities would loom. Relationships were teetering on lifetime commitments. Navigating the future felt dark in a way that a midnight hike feels dark. There isn't a light switch to flip to illuminate every rock that might stub your toe. Rather, there are a few glimmering stars that shed just enough light to let you know you are heading in the right direction. When you feel uncertain about the future, sometimes escaping to the mountains for a summer is the only way to make peace with the night sky.

For thousands of years, navigators and sailors relied on lights that could be seen from anywhere on the globe, to help them navigate long distances through the wilderness or across oceans. By day the sun was their guide, and by night the North Star led them forward. This was essential, because in order to avoid getting lost, it was imperative to know two things: where they were, and where they were going.

The North Star is the one star that is constant in its position in the night sky. It resides over the North Pole, while the other stars appear to circle around it. Interestingly, navigating by the North Star is considered much more reliable than consulting a compass, which is why when out on the sea, a clear dark sky and bright stars are even more helpful than calm seas on a sunny day.

As my friends and I lay under the stars, water lapping up on the sides of the dock, my new friend Marc taught me how to locate the North Star. Here is what I learned: The easiest method for finding the North Star is to locate the seven stars that make up the Big Dipper. From there, find the "pointer" stars; these are the two stars that form the outer edge of the Big Dipper. Once you've located the pointer stars, draw an imaginary line straight through the two stars of the Dipper edge toward the Little Dipper. The line will point very close to the handle of the Little Dipper. The brightest star in the Little Dipper is at the end of its handle. This is the North Star.

In many ways, that summer in Forest Falls felt like navigating uncharted waters. I had no idea what the future was going to look like, no idea what steps to take next. But Marc told me that if I was ever lost, to look to the North Star because it brought comfort to so many travelers who had gone before me. He assured me that the two most important things were to be able to honestly assess where I was, and then not to be afraid to move forward—even if I couldn't see the horizon. Apparently, looking up is better than looking ahead.

Do you ever feel like you don't know the next step to take? Like life is uncertain, or you can't see the path ahead of you? I feel like this most of the time. But what God continues to tell me is that there are whispers all around us, giving us clues. Rarely do we get to see the whole path laid out before us. Life is more like a hike in the dark where the stars come out to point us in the right direction.

For me there are two things that have acted as north stars as I navigate uncertainty.

Dreaming. A few weeks ago, I had a really strange dream. I was in a dance competition with Mr. Bedient, my fifth-grade teacher. He had spent the last twenty-five years of his life perfecting the Tango. I kept stepping on his toes. He fired me as his partner and chose my dog Oliver instead. Oliver turned out to be a very talented dancer. At this point, Snoop Dogg showed up. He and I hit it off right away. He thought I was hilarious. Mr. Bedient and Oliver ended up winning the competition, while Snoop Dogg and I cheered him on from Snoop's private bowling alley.

We all have weird dreams sometimes, right? Mostly dreams probably mean nothing and are purely our brain's way of sorting out the day. But sometimes we have other kinds of dreams.

Like when Joe and I needed to sell our house. I mean, a we-couldn't-make-our-next-mortgage-payment-needed-to-sell-now sort of sale. The house had been on the market for months, and offers kept falling through. One night I dreamed that God told me our house wouldn't sell because I had unfinished business with some friends in this town we were living in. I woke up in a cold sweat. We had a couple, who were friends, who had decided they felt hurt by me, so much so that they didn't want to be our friends anymore. I didn't feel like I had done anything wrong, so I dragged my feet in listening to the dream. Two weeks later, this couple and I happened to show up at the same park at the same time. I knew what I had to do. Pushing my ego aside, I went up to them and apologized for hurting them. We had a healing conversation.

They apologized for their part and a truce was negotiated. The next morning, we received a fax with an offer above our asking price.

A friend of mine named Emerson once told me that ever since he was a teenager, he has had occasional nightmares that are so intense he is certain there are spiritual matters taking place. Light-and-darkness type of stuff. I have another friend who, when faced with a difficult decision, prays before she goes to bed that her dreams will give her insight into the situation.

To indigenous tribes all over the world, the dream world is like church. Dreams are holy places where we can hear from the divine. The ancient world and biblical world knew a lot about dreams. God's story in the world is filled with wise men and women who listened to their dreams and knew how to interpret them. Different people have varying comfort levels with the whole dream discussion. You may be feeling like this whole topic is crazy talk. But from what I can see, our dream life can give us glimpses into the way forward. It is one way we can intentionally access the depths of knowing that our rational mind can't reach on its own.

Maybe tonight is the night to start asking for dreams. Dreams about your future, dreams about how to navigate a situation that is stumping you. God has used dreams to speak to his people throughout history. You are no exception.

Questing. Not long ago, we made a big move. We packed up three kids, a dog, and a U-Haul and drove through four states to live an adventure. We waved good-bye to best friends and family and hugged each other, knowing that adventures are good for the soul. We had no clue where we would live when we arrived at our destination; we only knew we needed to go.

Right before we left, my friend Michael reminded me of the ancient practice of questing. It was part trip, part ritual, in which spiritual seekers ventured into the unknown, confronted difficulties and dangers, and returned home with new understanding of themselves and the world. Known in some traditions as pilgrimage, questing could be an urge to explore one's spiritual roots, a desire for absolution, or a question that needs answering. The idea is that when you don't know what to do, maybe just do *something*. Leave what feels like home, figuratively and literally, and go somewhere you have never been before. And when you go, keep searching for the next step, even if you stumble. The goal is to ask questions, to look for answers in areas where you have never thought to go before. And when you find a gift or insight, to bring it back with you because it will help you on future journeys.

Are you open to letting yourself be guided? Is it time to embark on a quest? If your next step feels uncertain, if you are looking for answers, you are in good company. It is curious explorers and navigators just like you who have shown the rest of us there are new things to be discovered. Without people like you we would still believe the earth is flat.

So adventure on. Maybe it will be a quest that gives you direction for your future or a dream that points you in the right way. Whatever it is, make a move. Look up and locate the North Star. Pray for dreams and travel somewhere you have never been. And while you are doing *something*, be dazzled by a brilliant God who is always unfolding before us something bigger than ourselves.

The North Star will be out tonight. May it show you the way forward.

Q & R

1. At this season of your life, do you sense you know where you're going, or are you feeling a little lost?

2. Are you open to letting yourself be guided?

3. What are some of the whispering clues all around you about where you're headed?

4. Have you ever felt "led" by a dream?

5. What do you think about the suggestion, "When you don't know what to do, just do something"?

* * *

CHAPTER 28

Good Things Run Wild:
The Kingdom Comes

At seven o'clock on summer evenings the pasture out back smelled like clover.

And clover tasted like freedom.

When I was ten years old, I would saddle up my horse Royal for an early evening ride through the back pasture. From the barn, we would head west and make a left near the grapevines. As soon as we were through the metal gate, we knew we were free to run. Out of sight of parents or the farmer who lived next door, I would let out the reins, tap Royal's side with my heels, and we would gallop. The rhythmic three-step pattern of Royal's cadence felt like music—my own rebel yell. I would hunch my shoulders over so my face was close to his neck. His mane whipped my cheeks as we raced through the field so fast I could barely catch my breath. We were free to run.

Reaching the back of the field, the path narrowed, and Royal would slow to a walk. His breath was furious, panting from the sprint. My breathing mimicked his, but my breathlessness was the result of sheer exhilaration. Right before we reached the crooked part of the path where an old maple tree had fallen, I would hop out of the saddle to pick the pinkish-purple flowers that grew in patches just over the hill. Royal would graze on the tall grass, while

I plucked petals to taste the honey-flavored ends of the flowering clover.

Inevitably, Royal and I would lose track of time. We would linger too long in the tall grass, stars would brighten, and daylight would dim. My parents would send my brother out on the four-wheeler to remind us to come home. I would climb onto Royal's back, and we would reluctantly make our way home to the barn. The trip home was always slower, because freedom tasted too good to rush back to the ordinary. Together we plodded along the path and relished this magical time of day when sunlight and starlight mingled with ease.

It was this particular summer when I first learned that living in both sunlight and moonlight is where the freedom really happens. Fully welcoming both darkness and light feels like a sprint through the pasture—thrilling and just scary enough to remind you that you have breath in your lungs.

Many moons have passed since Royal and I ran through the pasture, but even all these years later, warm nights remind me that goodness is waiting to be found in all gradations of illumination. Sometimes we are looking for a path through the darkness and other times we are seeking a respite from blistering light. Whatever we are seeking, it seems to me that goodness is always waiting for us just up ahead, looking for an opportunity to run wild.

I was reminded of this recently when I stayed at a hotel in Boston. At the very front of the entrance by the big, swirling, circular doors was a small desk labeled "Concierge." For some reason, the concierge always intimidates me. I never really know what their job is, except what I assume it to be—a reservation-making, personal shopper for fancier, busier people than me. As I noticed the Concierge placard all shiny and fancy on the desk, it reminded me of a story my friend Jared once told me.

On his business cards, Jared has four titles that explain who he is. Instead of the typical titles like Project Manager or Director of Marketing, Jared's identifying titles are Clergy, Cocktail Maker, Curator, and Concierge.

Concierge? Seriously? Who wants to identify as a ticket purchaser for the hoity-toity? I didn't get it.

Jared explained.

Concierge is a French word that means something much richer than the typical "doorman" translation that we assign it. In French, it actually means "keeper of the candles." The story goes that if you arrived at a kingdom at night, and the king was away or asleep or indisposed, the concierge's responsibility was to make sure your entry into the kingdom was afforded all the opportunities that the king would want you to have were he there to greet you himself. The concierge saw to it that there was light and life in the kingdom at all times. Even in the middle of the night, a warm fire would be stoked to offer comfort in the darkness. The concierge represented the king and worked to share the full experience of the kingdom with all who came near.

I hope in some small way that the words you have spent time with in this book, words that have been invited into your home to share late nights or a cup of tea, will serve as a concierge, a reminder of the goodness that the King intends for you. Because the truth is, the King is currently away, and we each have been tasked with serving as concierges for one another—charged with making sure that there is light and life and warmth, even in the dark. We are the ones who can light a candle and welcome one another in. For when we get a glimpse of goodness, we realize there is no need to fear. The kingdom has come, and it is good.

G. K. Chesterton wrote something I love. In the passage he is referencing Christianity, but if that isn't your frame of reference I still think you can find truth in it. He says, "And the more I considered Christianity, the more I found that while it had established a rule and order, the chief aim of that order was to give room for good things to run wild."[1]

Good things run wild.

Good things are not bound by constraints. They do not play by the rules that insist one half is good and the other is evil. Good can be found in both.

Light is separated from the darkness.

And it is good.

Both.

Stars explode.

Bodies are birthed.

Sunlight and moonlight mark days and seasons.

Tears and laughter weave minutes into memories.

Candles flicker in the dark, reminding us of the goodness of the King.

The kingdom has come.

And out back, behind the King's home, is a pasture that is wide and deep and free.

Go. Run.

Because living in both the sunlight and the moonlight means running free, unafraid of the dark, no fear of exposure to the light.

Taste the sweetness of clover. Draw near to the rhythmic song that has been carrying you.

This is our rebel yell.

We shout with confidence,

"The Light has come!"

The darkness will not overcome it.

It will define it.

And that is good.

Run wild and be starry-eyed.

---

1   G. K. Chesterton, *Orthodoxy*, Image Classics (Colorado Springs: Image, 2001), 176.

Q & R

1. Growing up, when did you taste and enjoy freedom?

2. Do you like the idea of being a concierge for your friends, family, and strangers in this world?

3. Where in your life do good things currently run wild?

4. Do you believe that goodness is looking for an opportunity to show up in both darkness and light in your life?

5. In light of this life examination you have done, what are the major themes you have seen emerge from the constellation of your light and dark experiences?

* * *

Acknowledgements

This is a book birthed in the dark. From late-night writing sessions after my kids were tucked in, to 3:00 a.m. early morning shifts when I couldn't sleep so writing seemed to be the best option. Almost every word that you find in this book found its place on the page under a night of glimmering stars. After spending so many days in the dark, I became acutely aware of, and grateful for, the ones who remind me what light and warmth feel like. The ones who make life deeper and richer and way more fun.

I will be forever grateful to editors extraordinaire Stephanie Smith and Carolyn McCready. These are two of the most brilliant and genuinely enchanting women I have ever met. One of the best parts of writing is getting to work with these two women. Stephanie, thank you for the weekend calls and your unending patience. Many thanks also to Londa Alderink and the entire marketing team at Zondervan. Thanks to Traci Mullins, who makes every word better with her skillful editing. And a huge hug of gratitude to Chris Beetham, a gifted copyeditor and skillful scholar.

Thanks feels inadequate to express all the feelings I have for the A-team. My coconspirators and adventurers, Joe, Joseph, Ellie, and Charlotte, being with you is my favorite part of any day. To my brother Charley and my mom Cindy, thank you for letting me tell our stories. Big love to Lacey and CJ, you have brought light and love to our family, and I couldn't love you any more if I tried. A million hugs to my grandpa Bill, whose example of faith and courage beacon us forward. To all the Schippers and Dawes, we have been gifted with quite a legacy of love.

To the Arioto crew, Ed, Gayle, Jordan, Ryan, Brandon, Lori, Robert, Jake, Josh, Amy, Ron, Emma, Ronny, and Hailey, thank you for sharing Joe and for your unending passion and pursuit of living life to the fullest.

To my team at MOPS, I am honored to work alongside you. Liz, thank you for obliging all my last-minute editing requests. To Jackie Alvarez, Emma Turnbull, Jackie Frohne, Greg Henry, Kelli Jordan, Jen Iverson, Hannah Littlefield, Bre Mertens, and Blake Talley, thank you for an endless supply of laughter and patience; you are the ones who are making the magic happen. Good things run wild. Additionally, thank you to TJ, Gayle, Di, Karen, Gina, Andrea, and Sherry, sitting around a table with you is a gift.

To Jody, Tom, and the entire Anthony clan, thank you for being family and including us in yours. You have been there for all the moments, and for that I am eternally grateful.

Thanks to friends who have shaped so many of our days, Jen and Brian Mahoney, Drea, Hal and Bowie Horrowitz, Kristen and Simon Pollard, Ryan and Ruth Meissner, the Murrays, Michelle and Ryan Blair, and our Mosaic San Diego Crew. Living life with all of you makes for the best moments.

Lastly, thank you to my dad, Charles McAvoy. While I was never able to say it to his face, I am deeply thankful for the many lessons he taught me, including to always try my hardest, that horses are magical, and living big is always worth it.

About MOPS

You and I and the mom at the park and the mom in India—we have been placed in this time and space to raise the world together. Our purpose is the same even when our day-to-day experiences are different.

Being a mom is beautiful and hard, and we get that sometimes you just need a safe space to breathe. A place to get some encouragement that what you are doing matters. MOPS is a movement helping women around the world to become leaders in their community, to feel more equipped as moms, and to bring us all together to support one another.

Visit **mops.org** to read the blog,
learn more, and connect with a group meeting near you.

* * *